Never Mind the Burdocks
A YEAR OF FORAGING IN THE BRITISH ISLES
SUMMER / JUNE - AUGUST
by Emma Gunn
Published by Bramble and Bean Publishing House,
December 2020. First Print.
Printed and bound in the South West, UK.
Copyright Emma Gunn 2020
ISBN ISBN-13 : 978-0992969318

Designed and print managed by
Leap a certified B Corporation.
www.leap.eco

nevermindtheburdocks
@Nmtheburdocks
@emmatheforager
emma@nevermindtheburdocks.co.uk
nevermindtheburdocks.co.uk

FOREWORD

Written by Roger Phillips

WHEN THE LAST TREE IS CUT DOWN, THE LAST FISH EATEN, AND THE LAST STREAM POISONED, YOU WILL REALIZE THAT YOU CANNOT EAT MONEY.

A traditional Cree Indian saying

This is Emma's 4th volume in her all-encompassing survey of edible plants for foragers. Foraging is as old as man, yet in our post-industrial world the skills have largely become lost. Survival on foraged food is difficult, but in these volumes Emma Gunn opens up the whole field for the reader to explore.

Emma gives us a breadth of knowledge and ideas for all the different forms of edible additions to our diet that can be found in the wild. I commend her for including fungi and mushrooms in her work, for many others writing on this subject avoid them, as being too difficult or too dangerous. Emma also includes seaweed, for which she deserves fulsome praise, as we, an island nation, tend to ignore the food potential that surrounds us; the Japanese with a very similar sort of island habitat use seaweed continuously and Emma doesn't hesitate to include it in her detailed survey of all the treats that eating from the wild offers. The greatest treat of all, to my mind, is the satisfaction of being able to provide food for yourself or your family from nature, using your own knowledge and resources. How much more fun it is to spend time shopping in the wild, woodland, moorland or seaside, than yet another dreary visit to the supermarket.

Roger Phillips
Eccleston Square
March 2020

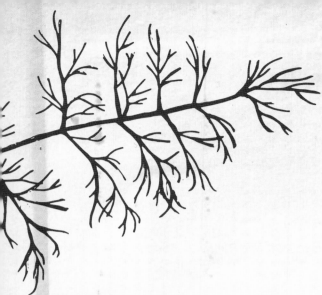

With thanks to...

Mum, Pip, Lowen, Matt Hocking (I owe you for all your late nights), Tim Pettitt my fungus guru, Orlagh Murphy, Chevonne Johanning, Roger Phillips for the foreword (the legend), Sally for being the best sister in the whole world, Kerry Woodfield, Matt Vernon, Lisa Cutcliffe and Mark Williams for your support and help, food-guinea pigs and everyone else who has helped and supported me along this journey...

Dedicated to Lowen, my positive, loving, thoughtful and constant ray of light.

Designed and produced as responsibly as possible by Leap, a certified B Corporation design agency based in Cornwall, creating branding, design for print and website's for projects all over the world. Their studio is powered by 100% renewable energy, they only use recycled or sustainable materials where possible in their creative work. www.leap.eco #designforchange

This book has been printed on 130gm2 silk (FSC Mix 70%) for the text pages and 350gm2 silk (FSC Mix 70%) for the cover. Using vegetable based inks and has a Carbon Neutral footprint.

CONTENTS

HOW TO USE THIS BOOK

On each day there is an edible item, be it a plant, mushroom, fish or other, starting with its scientific name. This is crucially important as this can truly identify the plant, fish or otherwise. The reason it is so important is that there can be many common names for one plant for example but only ever one scientific name which is universally used. If using a plant for food or medicine you can imagine how important it is that you have the right plant because this could be the difference between life and death!

Next is the common name, this will aid you in recognising the plant, fish, shellfish, seaweed or mushroom. This may not be what you call it but this is a great example of why the scientific name is needed.

A synonym is an 'old' scientific name used for the plant which may be what you know the plant as but has been updated due to perhaps its physiology, chemical make-up or otherwise.

The name origin is where its scientific name or common name comes from. I love this part as it can tell you a lot about where something is from, who discovered it, its colour, texture, growth patterns for example annual, biennial, perennial, in what season you would find it, the shape of it, where you would find it… the list is endless. This isn't just Latin but it can be a melange of many languages including Greek, Sanskrit, Old English, Germanic, etc.

The family of a plant is a group that pulls together characteristics that link many plants. For example the Brassicaceae family, otherwise known as the mustard family is simply a group of plants that all produce flowers with 4 petals in a cross shape and contain sulphur compounds. Sometimes, just knowing this can help with understanding the plant and how you can recognise it or how you can eat it.

Where it's found and edible part are self-explanatory. Where it's found is absolutely crucial for fungus forays as mushrooms are extremely specific so if you know a certain species likes growing only under beech trees, then you will not have discovered it under perhaps an oak. Edible part can be just as important as there are certain plants where it is safe to eat the young shoots but the fruits are seriously poisonous.

Edibility rating spans from 1-5, 1 being edible but pretty poor tasting and 5 is for the most tasty foraged food. This is my rating so you may disagree with the number I have given at times but everyone's taste buds are different so feel free to change the number to suit yourself.

Cautions are a guide as to what possible issues people may have with this item, for example if you are on any medication, pregnant or suffer from any health issues, then this will guide you as to whether this plant is safe for you to eat or not. This is something you need to do with food in general as people have allergies, some need to avoid certain foods for health issues, etc.

Where I have food ideas, this is again to guide you as to which bits you can eat, a guide as to how to prepare them and hopefully something you can take and run with. This can work with the recipe if there is one - try the recipe and if you like it, you may feel more confident eating the foraged food and trying it in your own recipes or day to day food. As I have learnt, do it gradually. I have tried a fully foraged meal before and been really disappointed! Try a little at a time or try to cook the item simply to see if your taste palate likes it.

Other info is to show that there are more to plants than meets the eye and to show they play and have played an important role in the life of humans for many centuries. This can be anything from medicinal uses to building materials.

Finally the last two titles are lookalikes and month span. For lookalikes this is to guide you away from possible similar plants that do more harm than good - have you seen 'Into the Wild'? Some plants, mushrooms, etc can look so similar but with one small difference can mean the difference between being very sick to having a tasty meal. Month span is to show you how long the foraged item is available for. This can be to help you eat it at its best or if it is shellfish, then to help you avoid them when it is their breeding season or when they are most likely to pick up bacteria in the warmer months that may cause you stomach upsets. (With plants, roots are best in autumn and winter as this is when they are storing their starches and sugars so during this period, the flowers, leaves or shoots tend to taste quite bitter as the plant is putting its energy into seeing it through the winter).

TIPS ON FORAGING

Any wild food must be treated as any new food which may cause allergies in certain people and not others - try out a little first and if no allergic reaction after a good length of time, then try more.

MUSHROOMS:

- There is no difference between mushrooms and toadstools, except people tend to call edible fungi 'mushrooms' and poisonous or toxic ones 'toadstools'.
- When picking fungi, ideally use a knife to harvest so you leave the mycelium (roots) behind so it can keep producing more fungi. Think of picking fungi like picking an apple off of a tree where the main part of the tree is underground.
- Fungi species need to be kept separate from each other in case there is a toxic one in the batch. Fungi can potentially contaminate other fungi.
- There are no rules of thumb that tell you whether a fungus is safe or not, so for example you can't tell if a fungus is safe or not by its gill colour.
- Only eat fungi when you are 100% sure what it is - consult a good guide, ask an expert, be certain and be safe.

Identify a fungus by looking at all of the below...
- Where it is growing - field, specific tree species, dead wood, etc.
- What time of year you find it
- Does it have a smell
- What colour is it
- Does it have a volva (egg shaped sac from which the stem grows)
- What do the gills look like
- Spore print
- Cap size
- Does it bruise when cut or pressed
- Does it have a ring on the stem

Once you have checked through all of these and it points at one specific edible fungus, then try it in small quantities as you may be allergic to it.

ROOTS:	• You can only uproot plants if you have the landowner's permission and as long as it is not a rare or endangered species. • If you dig up roots, then remember that plant will die. Only pick prolific plants.

FRUITS & BERRIES:	• Fruit colour does not identify whether it is safe or not. Raspberries, hawthorn fruits and rowan berries are all red, where edible black fruits include sloes, blackberries and black currants. • Check the foliage of the plant before picking the fruit to help you identify the plant correctly. • Be aware that certain toxic fruiting plants are climbers such as briony and honeysuckle and can entwine themselves in other plants so be careful what you are picking. • Leave plenty for wild life to eat. • Only harvest what you will eat.

LEAVES:	• Harvest edible leaves from a clean source and do not pick anything that is less than perfect. Imperfections can be caused by herbicide sprays, soil pollutants, insect damage, etc. • If picking edible plants that live in or by water, check the water quality and water source. Plants such as watercress can contain liver fluke from sheep which can be destroyed by cooking. • Leave most plants and especially shoots behind so the plant can photosynthesize - with very few leaves, the plant will struggle to grow. • Remember there can be lookalikes of plants so use your senses - if the plant is meant to be fragrant, smell it. If rough, feel it. If shiny, have a look, etc.

FLOWERS:
- Leave plenty of flowers on a plant for insects to feed on, for pollination but also for fruits to harvest later in the year.
- Pick flowers when it is sunny to get the best flavour or fragrance from them, for example honeysuckle flowers for making syrup or wine.
- Only pick what you need and will use.
- Don't pick rare or endangered flowers.

SEAWEEDS:
- Pick seaweeds using scissors so it can regrow.
- Sea creatures use seaweeds to hide and live in so take sparingly.
- Only harvest perfect looking species.
- Only harvest seaweeds that are attached to rocks rather than washed up on the shore. The seaweed may have been out at sea for ages before being washed up so the quality of it as a food is diminished.

TIDES:
- Respect the sea. Purchase a tide timetable for the area you will be foraging as the tides differ all around our coast.
- Keep an eye on the tides - you don't want to be cut off by the incoming tide and always have an escape route. You may be trapped on land for example on rocks but with no way to get back to safety.
- At low tides, weever fish bury themselves in the sand where unsuspecting people may stand on them and the fish injects venom into the person's foot. A way of avoiding this is to wear suitable footwear at low tides if paddling in shallow water. If you do get stung, put the affected area in as-hot-as-you-can-handle water without scalding yourself.

CLIFFS:	• Do not get too near the edge of a cliff. There is the potential to fall but also there may be very little ground beneath you, for example a cave. • When harvesting plants on or near a cliff, be aware that the cliff may not be stable and there is always potential for a landslip. • Do not attempt to climb up a cliff for wild food - the likelihood is you can find the same plant in a safer place. You do not want to cause unnecessary damage to the environment or yourself.

WEATHER:	• Dress suitably for the weather or take provisions with you if you are going to be out for a long time. • If you are going to be out for a while in the cold, wear a hat and gloves and keep warm. Wear suitable shoes - if wearing wellies, wear thick socks. • If it is warm and sunny, protect your head to limit the likelihood of getting sunstroke. Wear sun cream, take a long sleeved top with you and if you are out in the evening, the temperature can drop so take warm clothes with you. • As this is the UK, the weather can change for the worse quite quickly. Take wet weather gear with you just in case!

As a rule of thumb...
Young tender leaves and spring flowers are available in spring
Flowers and berries are available in summer
Autumn is good for the majority of fungi, fruits and nuts
Winter is when roots are at their best as the plant is storing sugars

This is not definitive but a very rough guide.

SCRIPT FOR MY TEDx TALK

The apocalypse is coming. Are you ready for it?

What will happen in an apocalypse? No electricity? Zombies from a chemical spillage? Contamination? Rising sea levels? (A virus???)

Why am I asking you this? My name is Emma Gunn and I'm here to help you survive.

One thing I do believe is that whatever the disaster, people tend to work together more often than not. We help each other, support each other and give… and here's my gift to you – 5 tips to surviving an apocalypse.

Tip 1, common sense

When it comes to foraging, don't eat anything you aren't 100% sure of. It is not worth the risk.

Leave plenty behind – you aren't the only one trying to survive. It is really easy to over-harvest but make sure there's plenty left for wildlife, for other humans and also if it's leaves you're picking, make sure the plant has plenty left to photosynthesize.

Collect food from a clean source. This may become increasingly difficult if there is a chemical spillage during our apocalypse but keep it in mind. If you are collecting shellfish, never pick after rainfall as the land will be leeching potential pesticides into the sea and therefore absorbed by these filter-feeders. Certain plants and seaweeds can thrive in contaminated soil such as gutweed and plants in the goosefoot family so be wary when foraging.

Since 1981 there has been a law which states you can't up-root anything without the landowner's permission but perhaps this rule may go out of the window. Again, this goes back to common sense as you need to keep as many food sources growing as possible. Roots are a great source of carbohydrate and starch, especially in the autumn and winter as the plant is arming itself to survive. Some plants provide bitters for digestion, natural sugars from fruits and berries… even seaweeds such as sugar kelp have high amounts of mannitol, a naturally occurring sugar. In shellfish and seaweeds you can find vitamin B12, calcium in leafy brassicas… it is all there for us to sustain ourselves. On a fundamental level, plants provide you with what you need at the right time of the year – starches and carbs to see you through the winter, new shoots and leaves in the spring providing vitamins and minerals, and antioxidants from fruits and berries through the summer.

Don't eat animals with 3 legs.

Last common sense tip – respect the elements. The weather can change quickly so make sure you are dressed appropriately, wear sensible shoes especially if you are exploring a rocky shoreline, get a tide timetable to check high and low tides and stay away from cliff tops when there's a hurricane!

Tip 2, arm yourself with knowledge

This may sound obvious but I want to delve a little deeper to help you with this.

I love the inclusivity of botanical names... yes inclusivity! When I was growing up, we moved country every 5 years. At the age of 11 we moved from Singapore to Chester and during the move I stumbled across a book called 'A book of Pot-Pourri', by Gail Duff. This was what started it all off... I'd always had an interest in plants but this sparked my fascination for 'plants with a use'. I taught myself hedgerow medicines and with the help of Latin, the names stuck.

Colloquial names are fine in their own areas – my Great Granny would send Dad, his brothers and cousins out picking sampeth and soursobs, aka marsh samphire (*Salicornia europaea*) and sorrel (*Rumex acetosa*). Dad knew what he was looking for. Common names serve a purpose but they're not universal.

With Victorian plant hunters introducing exotics and our climate changing, the diversity of what we can grow is getting broader and broader but something that can help with this is the universal botanical language. Plant names can tell us so much – about colour, where they grow, how they grow, if they are edible, useful... even if they are medicinal. Botanical names are also called 'Latin names' but they are often made up of any combination of Latin, Greek, Sanskrit, Old Germanic, Celtic, Hindi and so on.

One of my favourites is *Lamium galeobdolon* – *galeobdolon* means 'smells like a weasel'!

Other useful knowledge – what can you make? Can you make weapons? Can you fish? If you don't know how to, get friendly with someone who does and learn from them. Can you tie knots??
It is worthwhile learning a few medicinal plants – yarrow to stop bleeding, feverfew for headaches, meadowsweet to use instead of aspirin, plantain for bites...

Tip 3, read the land

The landscape can give us so much and we just have to scratch the surface for it to give us clues on survival. If you can recognize channeled wrack seaweed, you will never be cut off on a rising tide because it grows in the splash zone and the tide never comes up any further than this grows. If you find a patch of field mushrooms on a cliff top, look further inland with your back to the sea because the onshore winds carry the spores and therefore more mushrooms can be found. (If you follow the moons phases, you make the most out of collecting seaweeds because during a full moon you get spring tides meaning at low tide you will be able to harvest seaweeds that normally grow in subtidal zones such as sea spaghetti and sugar kelp.) Look

up, look down – I look everywhere when I'm out on a walk, especially the ground because I may spot a scattering of hazelnuts or a cluster of ash keys so I therefore know what trees are above me, no doubt laden with more delicious edibles.

Recognizing certain plants can help you spot where there might be a hidden stream or water source, such as marginals like water mint (*Mentha aquatica*) or toxic plants such as hemlock water dropwort (*Oenanthe crocata*).
In reverse, if you look for specific habitats such as estuaries, heathland or deciduous woodland, you'll have an idea of what plants you could find there. (This will become second nature pretty quickly and after a while you won't realize you are reading the landscape.)

You will start to build an edible 'map' in your head and so will return to the same favourite spots year after year, during certain months to get the best pickings. This may be your only weakness when it comes to surviving the apocalypse but only if it is a zombie apocalypse and they are the smart type who can predict where you're going to be and when! Mix it up and keep exploring new areas to keep them on their gangrenous toes.

Tip 4, don't get complacent
Complacency could get you killed.
Run fast.
Don't get comfortable with common names as they are often misleading and as I mentioned before, common names can vary so much but there is only one botanical name. As an extreme, misidentification could lead to poisoning yourself.

Any idea what 'bruisewort' or 'boneflower' is? It's more commonly known as daisy (*Bellis perennis*). Here's some confusing common names I want you to try out... any idea what blue rocket is? Monkshood, (*Aconitum napellus*), the Australian carrot fern? Hemlock, (*Conium maculatum*) ...dwayberry? Deadly nightshade, (*Atropa belladonna*).

Mushrooms are massively difficult if you don't use a mental check list for identification. Unfortunately there are no 'rules' to follow when it comes to whether a mushroom is edible or not. You can't just go on smell, gill colour, what colour it goes when cut or bruised... but these characteristics can all help with identification. What you can do is work out the genera but from that point you need to be specific.

Here's a quick quiz on mushrooms I like to call Edible or Deadible! Everyone stand up. Now raise your hand if you think...

Weeping widow is edible? Who thinks Deadible? – edible but bitter
Yellowdrop milkcap is edible? Who thinks Deadible? – deadible (poisonous)
Deceivers is edible? Who thinks Deadible? – edible, even raw

Death trumpet/Trompette des morts is edible? Who thinks Deadible? – edible
Brown Rollrim is edible? Who thinks Deadible? – was once believed to be
edible but it is actually an accumulative poison.

"All fungi are edible. Some fungi are only edible once" Terry Pratchett
This is true to some extent but the word 'edible' literally means 'non-toxic',
but you get the sentiment.

STICK WITH WHAT YOU KNOW
FIND A GOOD GUIDE AND ID BOOKS... Hire ME?
My mission is to arm people with knowledge, break down barriers,
inspire people to have a go themselves and do it with the least impact on
the environment.

When I mentioned the mushroom checklist, when I come across a species I
will check to see if...

The fungus has gills, pores, tubes or spikes. I look at the colour, see what it is
growing in or on (such as deadwood, a birch tree, grassland). I smell it, touch
the cap – is it slimy? I'll squeeze the stem and break it to see if it changes
colour. Does it have a ring on the stem or a swollen base? Do the gills run
down the stem, are they crowded, do they exude a milky substance? All of
these questions are helping me narrow it down as to what I have found.

When collecting fungi, it's best to collect them in a basket. Try and keep
fungi separate, especially if you are collecting some for ID. If one mushroom
is toxic, it has the potential to cross-contaminate if perhaps a piece of gill
breaks off and gets lodged in an edible.

Don't let this put you off. I suggest you focus on the top 10 edible and most
easily identifiable mushrooms. When you are happy with these, expand your
knowledge at a rate you find comfortable.

Keep running shoes on at all times, just in case the zombies are fast... my
Dad would keep his running shoes on when he was experimenting with
chemical reactions in the shed as a boy, just in case one went wrong!

tip 5, we don't have to just survive... we can thrive and enjoy it!
The flavours we get from wild food can be incredible.
 There is such a primal joy from being out in the elements all year round,
our bodies benefit from eating seasonally, getting scratched when picking
blackberries is part of the adventure, seeing kids explore wildlife, etc.
You can be a baddass forager but you don't have to be – this is for everyone.
It doesn't matter where you live or who you are.... this is for you.

Follow my rules and we can survive the apocalypse.
But we don't have to wait for an apocalypse... let's do this now.

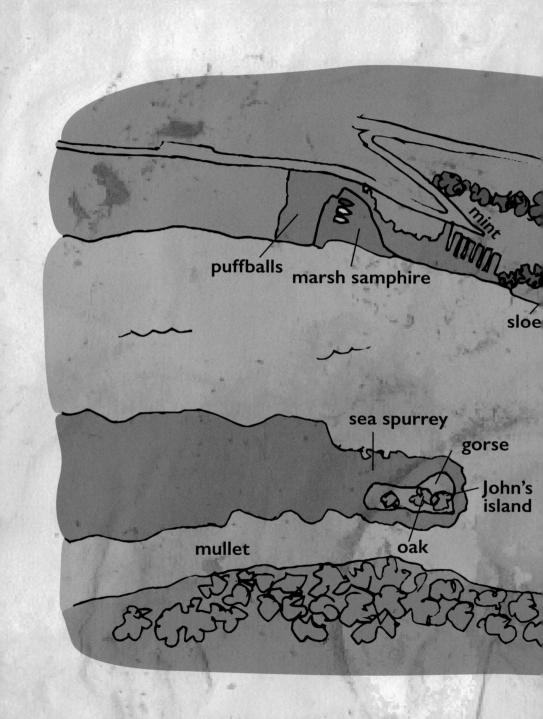

JUNE

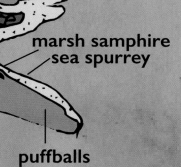

marsh samphire
sea spurrey

puffballs

Jo's spa pools

WALNUT
Juglans regia

NAME ORIGIN:	*Juglans* is the old Latin name for walnut tree, and *regia* means royal. It is also possibly from Jovis glans, meaning Jupiter's nuts!
FAMILY:	Juglandaceae

EDIBLE PART:	Leaves, sap (for the nuts see November 11th), unripe walnuts
EDIBILITY RATING:	2
WHERE IT'S FOUND:	Deciduous woodland, parks and gardens
CAUTIONS:	Avoid if you have nut allergies

LOOKALIKES:	Walnut leaves are pinnate, which means feather-like. Other trees with similar shaped leaves are ash *Fraxinus excelsior,* hickory *Carya* sp., pecan *Carya illinoinensis* and black locust *Robinia pseudoacacia* but the only one you will come across in the wild in the UK is ash. Ash has 7 similar sized leaflets where a walnut can have 9+ leaflets and clusters of pendulous winged 'keys'.
FOOD IDEAS:	Walnut leaf wine, tea from leaves, pickled unripe walnuts. Whole walnuts are good for pickling in June but beware, they stain your skin black in the process! To pickle them, cut the whole fruits in half or quarters to check the shell hasn't hardened and brine them for 10 days to 2 weeks. Drain off the brine and pour pickling vinegar over them and store for a few months before eating.
MONTH SPAN:	In leaf from May, flowers and unripe fruits in June.
OTHER INFO:	This is one of the last trees to emerge from its winter slumber. The tree is rich in tannins which can help reduce perspiration if you make an infusion of the leaves and use it as a wash. Walnut leaf also helps with expelling worms and soothing skin conditions such as eczema, psoriasis and athlete's foot, as well as making a good hair rinse for dark hair.

WALNUT LEAF WINE

4.5ltr young walnut leaves
1.3 kg sugar
2 tsp citric acid
4.5ltr water
1 packet wine yeast
1 packet wine nutrient

Boil 2.8ltr water with the sugar until the sugar has dissolved, then pour it over the walnut leaves, leaving it to infuse for 24 hours. Strain into a demi john or fermenting bucket with an air lock on it and add the rest of the ingredients. Shake it up then top it up with the rest of the water, seal and leave to ferment in a warm place. When the air lock has stopped bubbling and the liquid has cleared, rack it (which means bottling them and laying the bottles on their side). Leave them like this for 2 months, rack again, leave for 3 months then enjoy!

SALSIFY CHIPS

As many salsify roots as you can get (with permission to uproot them from the landowner),
sunflower oil to deep fry
sea salt
kitchen roll

Pretty simple, wash and peel the salsify roots, chopping them into chip size pieces. Heat the oil, testing with a cube of bread – when dropped in, it should rise to the surface and turn golden. When the oil is ready, put the salsify chips in (careful with the hot oil) and remove with a slotted spoon when golden. Put onto a plate with kitchen roll to blot off excess oil, then sprinkle with sea salt.

OTHER INFO

This has become one of my favourites and the first time I spotted it, it was such a surprise to find as we often go to this particular beach and have never seen it before (I guess we have never been at this time of year to catch it flowering). It has such a beautiful purple flower nestling within its long green pointy calyx. You can use the sap from the roots like chewing gum

SALSIFY

Tragopogon porrifolius

SYNONYM:	*Tragopogon sinuatus*
NAME ORIGIN:	The genus comes from the Greek word *tragos* meaning goat, and *pogon* which means beard as it has silky 'beards' on the seeds. The species name *porrifolius* means leek-leaved (in French, a leek is 'poireau'… was Agatha Christie's famous Belgian detective actually called Hercules Leek?
FAMILY:	Asteraceae
EDIBLE PART:	Root, seed, flower, flower bud, stem, leaves
EDIBILITY RATING:	4
WHERE IT'S FOUND:	Coastal, in dunes

LOOKALIKES:	The most similar plant is *Tragopogon pratensis* (goat's beard) but that normally occurs in fields, meadows, pastures and has a yellow flower rather than a purple one (also edible in all the same ways)
MONTH SPAN:	Flowers from May - August, seeds ripen July - September
FOOD IDEAS:	Eat the roots cooked or raw which taste mildly like oysters. It is best to harvest the roots (with permission) from mid-autumn to spring, before the plant starts to flower. To cook the roots, peel them and put them in a bowl of cold water with a squeeze of lemon juice or vinegar to stop the roots from discolouring. Boil for about 20 - 30 mins and serve with butter (and lemon juice). The taste is similar to mild sweet potato. I have included salsify now as this is the best time to identify it from the purple flowers which you can also eat, as well as the flower buds (both raw or cooked), which are tasty and sweet. Pick an unopened bud and stem sporadically so you leave plenty behind, steam them until tender and serve with a little butter or Hollandaise… delicious. The seeds can be sprouted like cress and added to salads, as a garnish, etc. Goat's beard (*Tragopogon pratensis*) is cooked and prepared exactly the same way

SWEET CICELY
Myrrhis odorata

NAME ORIGIN:	**The genus comes from the Greek word *myrrha* meaning fragrant and *odorata* means fragrant or scented**
FAMILY:	**Apiaceae**
EDIBLE PART:	Leaves, unripe and ripe seeds, roots
EDIBILITY RATING:	3
WHERE IT'S FOUND:	Hedgerows, grass, hillsides, by rivers and streams

LOOKALIKES:	Hemlock! Hemlock (*Conium maculatum*) has purple blotches and no hairs on its stem where sweet Cicely never has purple blotches but does have hairs. Sweet Cicely has plenty of leaves up its stem which are often pale on the underside and have white blotches on top, not to mention the smell of aniseed (hemlock smells like mouse wee)
	Cow parsley *Anthriscus sylvestris* has really similar leaves to sweet Cicely but the aniseed smell of sweet Cicely will confirm which it is, plus sweet Cicely seeds are very long. Be careful with eating cow parsley as it can cause allergic reactions in some people
MONTH SPAN:	Flowers May - June, seeds ripen July - August
FOOD IDEAS:	The leaves make a delicious tea which is a good digestive aid; the seeds can be used as a flavouring. The root can be cooked and eaten as a vegetable. The leaves and seeds can be used to sweeten and temper the tartness of rhubarb and gooseberries. The leaves are great with beetroot, scallops, salmon and mixed with crème fraîche as a sauce

OTHER INFO:	Sweet Cicely contains anethol which gives the fragrance of aniseed, which stimulates all glands such as saliva, digestive juices and milk production. Seeds and leaves are good as a furniture polish! Just rub it on to wood, especially oak, then buff with a polishing cloth

SALMON AND SWEET CICELY EN CROUTE
(Serves 2)

1 pack of puff pastry
2 salmon fillets skinned (and
boned if necessary)
1 tub of low fat cream cheese
2 good handfuls
sweet Cicely leaves
Seasoning

Preheat the oven to 180 degrees C. Roll out the puff pastry to about 4mm thick. Cut in half - depending on the size of your salmon fillets and the size of the puff pastry, you may get more 'en croutes' out of this. Place your salmon fillet on the puff pastry like you're making a pasty, then put a generous dollop of cream cheese on the salmon, finely chop the sweet cicely and sprinkle that on top with the seasoning. Pull the pastry over to seal with water or milk, pressing the edge with a fork or crimping it. With a fork or skewer, make a couple of holes on top, brush with milk or egg yolk if you wish then bake in the oven for 30-40 minutes or until a rich golden colour and the salmon is cooked if you push a skewer into the middle and it comes out hot to the touch.

GOAT'S RUE
Galega officinalis

SYNONYM:	*Galega persica, Galega tricolor, Galega bicolor*
NAME ORIGIN:	The Greek word *gala* means milk and *ago* (ega) is 'to lead' as it was used as a fodder for goats.
FAMILY:	Fabaceae

EDIBLE PART:	Leaves
EDIBILITY RATING:	2
WHERE IT'S FOUND:	Roadsides, scrubland, woodland, marshland, meadows
CAUTIONS:	There are reports that this plant could be toxic to mammals but it is fed to goats to increase their milk flow
LOOKALIKES:	It looks quite similar to vetch and liquorice, but only due to the leaf shapes being typical of the pea/legume family (Fabaceae). Vetch *Vicia* sp. has tendrils for climbing and scrambling, Liquorice *Glycyrrhiza glabra* has purple to pale blue pea-like flowers where goat's rue has pink slightly shaggy looking flowers
MONTH SPAN:	Flowers June - July, seeds ripen August (hz 4)

FOOD IDEAS:	Have a go at cooking the leaves like spinach. It supposedly curdles milk so you could try to make cheese!
OTHER INFO:	The plant contains galegine that reduces blood sugar levels (when the alkaloid galegine is isolated from this plant it is useful in treating diabetes)

SCOTS LOVAGE
Ligusticum scoticum

NAME ORIGIN:	*Ligusticum* is Latin meaning from Liguria which is a region in Italy (lovage *Levisticum officinale* grows profusely there). *Scoticum* means from Scotland
FAMILY:	Apiaceae
EDIBLE PART:	Leaves, stem, seeds, root
EDIBILITY RATING:	3
WHERE IT'S FOUND:	Sunny, rocky coastline in the North, growing out of rocky fissures, especially in Scotland
LOOKALIKES:	Scots lovage looks like a cross between alexanders *Smyrnium olusatrum* and lovage *Levisticum officinale*
MONTH SPAN:	(hz 4) in leaf from about April, flowers June - August, seeds ripen September – November

FOOD IDEAS:	Eat the roots raw or cooked (with permission to dig them up from the land owner), the leaves and shoots raw or cooked and use the seeds like black pepper. It is a good idea to dry out the seeds a little on a low temperature in the oven so you can use them in a pepper grinder. The stem and leaves taste quite like celery. Try chopping the leaves and adding them to pasta dishes and soups. You can eat and prepare them exactly the same way as alexanders *Smyrnium olusatrum*
OTHER INFO:	Melanie, this one is for you to look out for! Scots lovage has good nutritional value and contains vitamin C

WHITE MUSTARD
Sinapis alba

SYNONYM:	*Brassica alba, Brassica hirta*
NAME ORIGIN:	*Sinapis* comes from the Greek word for mustard and *alba* means white in Latin.
FAMILY:	**Brassicaceae**

EDIBLE PART:	Leaves, seeds, flowers
EDIBILITY RATING:	3
WHERE IT'S FOUND:	Crop fields, waste land
CAUTIONS:	If you have mustard allergies, then it is best to avoid. Some reports suggest that the plant is toxic when flowering but I have eaten the flowers and leaves when flowering with no ill effects.

LOOKALIKES:	White mustard looks similar to black mustard *Brassica nigra* as both have yellow flowers with 4 petals, but black mustard leaves are rougher and have a slightly purple stem.
MONTH SPAN:	(hz 6) flowers from June - August, seeds ripen July – September
FOOD IDEAS:	Eat the leaves raw or cooked, add flowers to salads for pungency, seeds can be sprouted and eaten, toasted or ground as a flavouring. Use the whole seeds for pickling.
OTHER INFO:	This is often grown as a fodder crop and is a useful ground cover crop in vineyards as it helps suppress soil borne diseases.

ROSY GARLIC

Allium roseum

NAME ORIGIN:	**The word *all* is Celtic for burning/pungent and *roseum* means pink.**
FAMILY:	**Amaryllidaceae**
EDIBLE PART:	Flowers, leaves, bulbils, bulbs.
EDIBILITY RATING:	4
WHERE IT'S FOUND:	Verges, roadsides, coastal, grassland, rocky slopes
CAUTIONS:	All alliums (onion and garlic family) are toxic to dogs
MONTH SPAN:	Flowers May – June

FOOD IDEAS:	Eat the raw flowers, the bulbils are delicious raw or cooked, the leaves are edible but can be stringy and the bulb can be eaten raw or cooked.
RECIPE	Use the rosy garlic bulbils instead of garlic in vinaigrette and use the pink flowers as a garnish. Use in any savoury dishes to replace garlic.
OTHER INFO:	I first spotted this on the side of the road at the top of Mevagissey, a lovely Cornish fishing village but a tip for the summer, do not attempt to drive through it!
	The flowers are so beautiful and delicate and make a great addition to a garden for aesthetic and culinary use. If you want to try, collect the bulbils (their equivalent of seeds) and sprout them.

BORAGE SANDWICH

(adapted from an Antonio
Carluccio recipe)

a squeeze of lemon
juice to serve
seasoning
2 borage leaves per serving
olive oil to fry
1 egg roughly per serving
grated parmesan
1 dessert spoon of cream
cheese
3 borage flowers, roughly
chopped
¼ tsp chilli flakes

First put the cream cheese, chilli flakes and borage flowers in a bowl and combine. In a separate bowl beat the egg. Warm the olive oil in a frying pan on a medium heat. Dip one leaf in the egg mix and put in the frying pan. Sprinkle the grated parmesan on the borage leaf that is frying and spoon the cream cheese mix into the centre, then dip the other leaf in the egg mix and lay it on top. When the bottom is golden brown, flip over and cook the top leaf - the heat will penetrate through and cook all of the egg and parmesan in the centre. Serve with lemon juice and season to taste.

EXTRA INFO: Starflower or borage oil is one of the best plants used for menopause as it is extremely high in gamma-linolenic acid (GLA) which helps balance out menopausal symptoms. I moved about a fair bit as a kid - no I wasn't a delinquent but we moved because of Dad's work. When I was 11, we moved from Singapore to Chester. With the moving came constantly making new friends and keeping myself entertained... one wet day in July I was in the spare room when I came across 'A book of Pot Pourri' by Gail Duff. You may think it sounds dull, but it covered so many old references to plant uses, both cosmetic and medicinal. One of the best ones with a beautiful drawing of a bath was borage and how steeping it in wine alleviates melancholy. Fab book, it even has the language of flowers in the back of it and that a civet cat produces a perfume fixative from its urine - perfect reading for a smutty 11 year old!

BORAGE (STARFLOWER)
Borago officinalis

SYNONYM	*Borago hortensis, Borago advena, Borago aspera*
NAME ORIGIN:	The old Celtic word borrach means courage as warriors were given it before battle. Steeped in wine it supposedly alleviates melancholy. *Officinalis* means 'of the apothecary's shop' referring to its medicinal properties.
FAMILY:	Boraginaceae
EDIBLE PART:	Flowers, leaves, seeds
EDIBILITY RATING:	4
WHERE IT'S FOUND:	Gardens, waste ground
CAUTIONS:	The plant (not the oil from the seeds) contains pyrrolizidine alkaloids that cause liver damage if consumed in large quantities, as do other plants in this family. Avoid if you have liver problems
LOOKALIKES:	Borage can look similar to young common figwort plants *Scrophularia nodosa* at first glance but borage leaves have a rough texture whereas common figwort is hairless and smells pretty unpleasant
MONTH SPAN:	(hz 7) flowers from June - October, seeds ripen July – October
FOOD IDEAS:	Try freezing the flowers in ice cubes and decorating salads, as a garnish or desserts and savoury dishes. Steam, boil or fry the leaves, add to dishes or tempura batter and deep fry. I once made an ice bowl with a mix of colourful flowers including borage which is really cool! Get two bowls, one bigger than the other. In the large one, pour water and add any flowers you want. Putting the smaller one inside the other and weighing down with a plate, you can create an ice bowl that you can serve chilled food in (quickly on a hot day before it melts!)

OX-EYE DAISY dog daisy

Leucanthemum vulgare

SYNONYM	*Chrysanthemum leucanthemum*
NAME ORIGIN:	The synonym *Chrysanthemum* comes from *chrysos* which is Greek for gold, *anthemon* means flowers, the synonym species and current genus *leucanthemum* means white flowered. *Vulgare* means common
FAMILY:	Asteraceae

EDIBLE PART:	Flowers, flower buds, young leaves, roots
EDIBILITY RATING:	3
WHERE IT'S FOUND:	Meadows, grassland, roadsides
LOOKALIKES:	Shasta daisy *Leucanthemum* x *superbum* looks similar but has much larger flowers and is cultivated
MONTH SPAN:	(hz 3) flowers June – August, leaves available almost all year

FOOD IDEAS:	The flowers are great raw, added to salads, dipped in batter and deep fried, the flower buds pickled or eaten raw, the roots can be eaten raw and the leaves raw – add to salads as they have a good flavour and are substantial
OTHER INFO:	The flower buds are reminiscent of pineapple, cucumber and angelica! Like a road side sweet! I love this and often munch on the leaves, flower buds or open flowers and always include it in my foraging walks. When I was pregnant, I could really taste the pineapple but on discussing this with my foraging groups only half would agree (perhaps they were humouring me?!). The leaves have a fresh parsley-like taste to them with a lovely sweet aftertaste

ASH KEY PICKLE

2 cups ash keys without stalks
6 cloves
10 black peppercorns or
Alexander seeds
10 dried ash keys seeds
(optional)
5 bay leaves
3 tbsp brown sugar
2 cups cider vinegar
a pinch of salt

Sterilize 2 jars with boiling water - you can pop them in the oven in a tray with water to really sterilize them if you wish. Put the ash keys in a saucepan and cover with water. Bring to the boil and reduce to a simmer for 10 minutes. Throw away the water and add fresh water, repeating the process. In a heat proof bowl over a saucepan with simmering water (bain marie - don't let the bowl touch the water) put the rest of the ingredients and heat through. Allow to simmer and leave to infuse for a couple of hours. Pack the ash keys into the jars and pour the spiced vinegar through a sieve over the keys. Screw on the lids with parchment to keep them well sealed and store for a minimum of 3 months. Serve with cheese and crackers.

OTHER INFO:

Ash wood is excellent for making guitars such as telecasters and Fender Stratocasters because of the fine quality and resilience. The disease ash dieback is caused by a fungus called *Hymenoscyphus fraxineus*. It has reached the UK from Europe and has been found in woodland in Suffolk and is now widespread throughout the UK. If you have ash trees on your land, check for dead branches, discoloured stems often in a diamond shape where a leaf was attached and blackening of leaves which often hang on the tree - contact the Forestry Commission as soon as possible if you suspect you have found it www.forestry.gov.uk

One of my favourite Agatha Christie Poirot stories is 'The Hollow'. This is where I first heard of Yggdrasil as one of the main suspects would draw it absentmindedly.

ASH
Fraxinus excelsior

NAME ORIGIN:	*Fraxinus* is Latin for ash tree, *frango* is Latin for 'I break' and the Greek word *phrasso* means to fence. In Norse mythology the tree of life is the almighty ash called Yggdrasil. The common name ash comes from the Old English 'aesc', meaning 'spear'.
FAMILY:	Oleaceae

EDIBLE PART:	Unripe fruit (ash keys), dried keys
EDIBILITY RATING:	3
WHERE IT'S FOUND:	Hedgerows, scrub, woodland
MONTH SPAN:	I have found the unripe keys from May, dried ones in autumn/winter
CAUTIONS:	It can cause dermatitis in people with sensitive skin
MONTH SPAN:	In leaf May - October, flowers April – May
FOOD IDEAS:	The unripe raw ash keys taste a little buttery, then bitter, followed by a heat in the throat - not unpleasant. The pickled ash keys take on the pickle flavour well and give a good texture to go with cheese. When you find dried ash keys, split them in half to get the seed out and use it as an unusual spice which has a woody, almost vetiver-like, warm spicy, slightly nutmeg flavour. Dry and grind them up, using them to flavour cookies or keep them whole and use as a pickling spice

FUMITORY
Fumaria officinalis

SYNONYM	*Fumaria pulchella, Fumaria diffusa, Fumaria cirrhata, Fumaria disjuncta*
NAME ORIGIN:	*Fumer* is French meaning to smoke, *Fumaria* is Latin for 'smoke of the earth' as it looks like red clouds like smoke on bare ground. Fumitory comes from *fume terra* literally meaning earth smoke which is another common name for this plant.
FAMILY:	Fumariaceae

EDIBLE PART:	Aerial parts
EDIBILITY RATING:	2
WHERE IT'S FOUND:	Gardens, arable land
CAUTIONS:	Avoid during pregnancy and breast-feeding, avoid if you suffer from fits, epilepsy or on medication for high blood pressure, contraindicated with glaucoma patients.
LOOKALIKES:	*Corydalis* has the same delicate leaves as they are in the same family but fumitory grows on bare soil and arable land where *Corydalis* tends to be cultivated, plus the flowers of fumitory are pale pink with dipped burgundy/black ends.
MONTH SPAN:	Flowers May - September, seeds ripen June - October (hz 5)

FOOD IDEAS:	Use the aerial parts (fresh or dried) as a curdling agent for milk.
OTHER INFO	Fumitory is used medicinally for various skin complaints such as eczema and acne, and taken as a tea for indigestion and liver conditions.
	In Cornwall we have an endemic annual called *Fumaria occidentalis,* otherwise known as western ramping-fumitory. This is the largest species of the fumitories and loves the warmer climate of Cornwall and the Isles of Scilly.

OTHER INFO:

Every bit of an allium can be eaten, but as they begin to flower, some parts can become slightly bitter and stringy, and certain varieties aren't as tasty as others. An allium I am fond of is *Allium tuberosum* with its tiny white star-like flowers as it works very well in a herbaceous border and has a long flowering period.

Near the Eden Project, there is a Methodist church called Leek Seed Chapel. It is so-called because an attempted robbery on collected church funds was botched. Gardener Stephens was up late reading by candlelight after having collected and sifted through a load of leek seeds. The pile of leek seeds made a convincing mound of gunpowder which Gardener Stephens threatened to set alight to if they didn't hand over any money the robbers had and then leave immediately! His quick thinking saved the church funds.

ORNAMENTAL ALLIUMS
Allium sp.

NAME ORIGIN:	**The word *all* means pungent or burning in Celtic**
FAMILY:	**Amaryllidaceae**

EDIBLE PART:	Flowers
EDIBILITY RATING:	4
WHERE IT'S FOUND:	Cultivated ground, gardens, coastal areas
CAUTIONS:	All alliums (onion and garlic family) are possibly toxic to dogs
LOOKALIKES:	There aren't really any lookalikes except *Agapanthus*, but they don't smell of garlic and are less prolific in the wild unless you live on the Scillies. Always do the sniff test!

MONTH SPAN:	Ornamental alliums flower from about May until September, depending on the variety. The pompom ones such as *Allium giganteum, Allium christophii, Allium* 'Gladiator' flower roughly May/June where one of the last garden varieties to flower is *Allium sphaerocephalon*
FOOD IDEAS:	Allium flowers can be used to decorate and garnish salads, soups, sandwiches, etc. Some flower buds can be pickled or eaten raw, some leaves can be eaten where others are a little stringy, eat the bulbils raw or cooked, try the unripe seeds fresh or dried and some have very tasty bulbs. Did you know that elephant garlic is actually wild leek bulbs (*Allium ampeloprasum*)?
RECIPES:	I love using different ornamental allium flowers for decorating, especially the iridescent purples such as *Allium christophii*

PINEAPPLE WEED
Matricaria discoidea

SYNONYM	*Artemisia matricarioides, Chamomilla suaveolens, Matricaria matricarioides, M. suaveolens, Tanacetum suaveolens, Santolina suaveolens, Lepidotheca suaveolens, Lepidanthus suaveolens*
NAME ORIGIN:	*Matricaria* possibly comes from the ancient Latin word *matrix* meaning mother and *caria* meaning dear, probably referring to the medicinal uses for mothers, for example as a galactagogue (promoting lactation) and post partum anaemia
FAMILY:	**Asteraceae**

EDIBLE PART:	Flower heads
EDIBILITY RATING:	4
WHERE IT'S FOUND:	Compacted ground, entrance to fields, waysides
CAUTIONS:	Some people can be allergic to this plant
LOOKALIKES:	It does look similar to chamomile but nothing else tends to grow in such conditions that looks the same and pineapple weed has no petals (ray florets) – crush and sniff the plant to help identify it if you are unsure

MONTH SPAN:	In flower March – October, long life span for an annual
FOOD IDEAS:	Use the flower heads raw or dried, steep them in boiling water to make a pineapple-scented tea, use the flower buds in cakes, cheesecakes, chopped up in icing, in salads and salsas
OTHER INFO	Pineapple weed tea can act as a mild sedative and helps reduce fevers. It has a fantastic flavour for such a tiny plant which remains when it is cooked – one of my favourites!

PINEAPPLE WEED CUPCAKES (MAKES 12)

2 tbsp chopped pineapple weed leaves and flowers
110g self-raising flour
110g caster sugar
110g butter
2 eggs
Milk

Buttercream icing
140g softened butter
280g icing sugar
Milk if required
Pineapple-weed flower heads for decorating

Preheat the oven to 180 degrees C. Line a muffin tin with muffin cases. Beat the sugar and butter together, beat in the eggs and fold in the flour. Add a little milk to get the mixture to dropping consistency then lightly stir in the chopped pineapple weed. Put the mixture into the cases and bake (between 10-30 minutes so keep checking). Meanwhile make the buttercream icing by combining the butter and icing sugar until smooth (add milk if you need to make the mixture thinner). Leave the cakes to cool then top with the buttercream icing. Decorate with a pineapple weed flower.

CAMASSIA
quamash, wild hyacinth
Camassia quamash

NAME ORIGIN:	*Camassia* is from the North American name quamash.
FAMILY:	**Hyacinthaceae**
EDIBLE PART:	Bulb
EDIBILITY RATING:	3
WHERE IT'S FOUND:	Grassland, cultivated
CAUTIONS:	Other plants in this family are highly toxic, such as hyacinths (which I hate and they hate me).
LOOKALIKES:	Do not muddle up the name wild hyacinth with hyacinths as a hyacinth bulb is extremely poisonous and can cause dermatitis. The same goes for bluebells – do not mistake them for bluebells!
MONTH SPAN:	Flowers May - June, seeds ripen July – August

FOOD IDEAS:	Eat the bulb raw or cooked. *Camassia quamash* has a delicious mild potato flavour and is really good baked with olive oil and sea salt. They look like sticky mini shallots.
RECIPE:	Cook them in place of potatoes to accompany a dish.
OTHER INFO:	*Camassia leichtlinii* can be eaten in the exact same way, also known as wild hyacinth. Camassias look stunning as a cut flower and make a great addition to a garden border.

NASTURTIUM
Tropaeolum majus

SYNONYM	*Cardamindum majus, Tropaeolum elatum, Tropaeolum hortense, Trophaeum majus*
NAME ORIGIN:	The Latin word *tropaeolum* means trophy as the flowers are like helmets and the leaves are like shields, both scenes of victory. The word nasturtium comes from *nasus tortus* meaning twisted nose, due to the hot pungent taste. *Majus* means major or large.
FAMILY:	**Tropaeolaceae**

EDIBLE PART:	Flowers, leaves, unripe seeds
EDIBILITY RATING:	3
WHERE IT'S FOUND:	Gardens, garden escape
CAUTIONS:	Avoid giving to children and infants. Avoid if you have kidney disease or gastrointestinal ulcers.
MONTH SPAN:	Flowers June - September, seeds ripen August - October (hz 9)

FOOD IDEAS:	Eat the leaves raw in salads or sandwiches as they have a real bite to them like watercress. The raw flowers can be used the same way. The unripe seed pods can be used like a caper substitute and eaten raw (really hot - I can't stand them!!) or pickle them in vinegar and use as you would capers.
OTHER INFO:	If you need to decorate anything like a pond, then nasturtium leaves do the job!

NASTURTIUM PESTO

50g feta (1/4 pack of feta)
2 tbsp pine nuts or flaked
almonds
1 clove of garlic
150g nasturtium leaves
140ml extra virgin olive oil
Seasoning

Toast the pine nuts or flaked almonds until turning golden, then remove from the heat. Put all the ingredients into a blender except the oil and seasoning and blitz, then drizzle the oil in whilst blitzing until you have the required consistency. Taste and season accordingly.

COMFREY knitbone
Symphytum officinale

NAME ORIGIN:	The word *sympho* means to come together as it speeds up the healing of broken bones, fractures, etc. *Symphytum* was named by Dioscorides and goes back more than 2000 years. *Officinale* means of the apothecary's shop.
FAMILY:	**Boraginaceae**
EDIBLE PART:	Leaves, roots
EDIBILITY RATING:	4
WHERE IT'S FOUND:	Shady areas, damp ground, near water, woodland edge, hedgerow, meadows
CAUTIONS:	Don't eat too much because it contains alantoin - avoid if you have liver problems. Large quantities consumed of older leaves can cause liver damage (but you'd have to eat a lot!)
LOOKALIKES:	Similar to borage (same family) but comfrey (*Symphytum* sp.) leaves are pointed and more slender, whereas borage leaves are rounded at the tip and a little broader. *Cynoglossum* sp. can look similar but the flowers look more like forget-me-not flowers whereas *Symphytum* sp. has drooping, tubular flowers
MONTH SPAN:	Flowers May - June, seeds ripen June - July (hz 5)
FOOD IDEAS:	Tempura battered and deep fried leaves - delicious! The flavour reminds me of growing up in Singapore. Eating the young leaves raw is also delicious - they are quite like cucumber without any bitterness but a tiny bit slimy. Cooked and wilted like spinach in dishes, goes well with peanuts. Peel and cook the roots in soups or roast to make a coffee substitute

This plant really does speed up the healing process of broken bones fusing them back together and reducing bruises. It can also contain vitamin B12 if grown in the right conditions - otherwise seaweeds are the only plant source of this vitamin. Vitamin B12 can be found in fermented products such as soya sauce and marmite - excellent for stimulating hair growth

COMFREY ALOO

Olive oil to fry (2 tbsp)
1 onion peeled and finely diced
2 cloves of garlic peeled and minced
1 thumb sized piece of ginger - peeled and minced
5 medium sized potatoes peeled and cubed into roughly 2cm cube pieces
4-5 good handfuls of comfrey leaves washed
1 large hot chilli
sea salt
a pinch of kalonji black onion seeds (nigella) or black mustard seeds
a pinch of cumin seeds
a pinch of ground turmeric
a pinch of garam masala

In a large pan heat the oil and add the onion, ginger and garlic, frying for a few minutes but be careful not to let the garlic and ginger burn. Add the remaining ingredients except for the comfrey leaves and fry, adding water to prevent sticking when necessary. Cook for about 10 minutes or until the potato is cooked right through. Add the comfrey leaves and stir well to coat them with the spice mix until they wilt. Serve.

CHICKEN OF THE WOODS

sulphur polypore
Laetiporus sulphureus

NAME ORIGIN:	*Laetiporus* means with bright pores and *sulphureus* means sulphur coloured as this fungus is yellow
FAMILY:	**Polyporaceae**

EDIBLE PART:	Mushroom
EDIBILITY RATING:	4
WHERE IT'S FOUND:	Chicken of the woods grows mostly on older trees especially oak as well as others, either dead or living. It can also be found on beech, sweet chestnut, yew, cherry, willow and eucalyptus
CAUTIONS:	Avoid picking if growing on yew trees. It must be cooked (don't eat raw)
LOOKALIKES:	Nothing really looks like this except *Phaeolus schweinitzii* which is a bracket fungus that grows on conifers and is hairy and a bit brown

MONTH SPAN:	Spring - autumn, especially June, September and October
FOOD IDEAS:	Parboiled and fried, add to casseroles. If you want to freeze for later use, wipe clean, chop into cubes and gently fry in butter, then freeze. You can also grill them and they make great satay

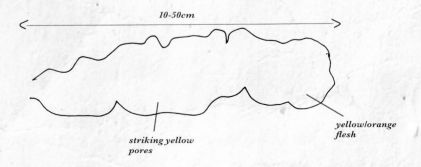

10-50cm

striking yellow pores

yellow/orange flesh

MUSHROOM RAGOUT WITH MASH

serves 4

1 oz butter
2 lb chicken of the woods mushrooms or a combination with others such as field mushrooms
1 tbsp plain flour
1/2 a glass of sherry
1/4 pt vegetable stock
1/2 pt double cream
1/2 a lemon
Seasoning
a good handful of tarragon or thyme

For the mash...
2 lb potatoes
Up to 10 fl oz milk
a knob of butter
and seasoning

Peel the potatoes and chop roughly into cubes. Put them in a saucepan, cover with water and bring to the boil. When boiling, reduce the heat slightly and cook until tender. Meanwhile wipe clean the mushrooms with a cloth - don't wash them, then chop into good sized chunks or thick slices. Melt the butter in a large frying pan and add the mushrooms, cooking them until they start to show a little colour. Sprinkle on the flour, stir well, cook for a minute, then add the sherry, vegetable stock, herbs and seasoning. Simmer for 15 minutes. (When the potatoes are cooked, drain and leave in the colander.) Add the lemon juice and cream to the mushrooms and simmer for 5 minutes - if the mixture is too thick, add a little water or stock to it. If the potatoes have gone cold, pour boiling water over them to reheat. Drain, then put back in the saucepan and add some milk until you're happy with the consistency, butter and seasoning and mash well. Serve together with greens. If you don't fancy mash, then use filo pastry as in the photo.

HONEYSUCKLE WINE

recipe adapted from the
Herb Society.

2 pints of honeysuckle
flowers
2 3/4lb granulated sugar
(or 2 1/2lb sugar for a less
sweet wine)
1lb raisins chopped
2 tsp citric acid
juice of 1 orange
2 fl oz lady grey tea (brewed
with 2 teabags and steeped
for 10 minutes)
6 pints of water
1 sachet champagne yeast
(or white wine yeast sachet).

Wash, remove the green parts of the flowers and shake dry. Put the flowers, sugar, raisins, orange juice, tea and citric acid in a fermenting bucket. Add boiling water and stir. Leave to cool until quite warm and add the wine yeast to activate it. Cover and leave it for 4 - 5 days in a warm room. Strain into a demi-john and top up to the neck with cold boiled water. Leave it to ferment for 3 months. By then it should be clear and ready for bottling. This really does taste like the essence of walking down country lanes with the heady aroma of summertime in your nostrils!

HONEYSUCKLE
Lonicera periclymenum

NAME ORIGIN:	Named after Adam Lonicer who was a German 16th century naturalist and the species name means to twine around. The species *periclymenum* comes from the Greek *periklymenon* who was a Greek argonaut and a shape-shifter
FAMILY:	**Caprifoliaceae**
EDIBLE PART:	Nectar and flowers
EDIBILITY RATING:	4
WHERE IT'S FOUND:	Hedgerows, woodland, scrub
CAUTIONS:	Only use the flowers as the rest is very poisonous. Symptoms are sleepiness, vomiting, dilated pupils, fear of light and then death! The fruits also contain saponins
MONTH SPAN:	(hz 4) flowers from May - September, fruits from July – October

FOOD IDEAS:	Suck the nectar from the flowers, eat the flowers in salads, as a garnish on puddings or make into a syrup. I have read conflicting reports on the berries where they are edible in small quantities and also that they are deadly poisonous… I suggest you AVOID!
OTHER INFO:	When woodbine is mentioned in poems, it is referring to a variety of honeysuckle

HOPS
Humulus lupulus

SYNONYM	*Humulus americanus, Humulus volubilis, Humulus vulgaris, Lupulus amarus*
NAME ORIGIN:	*Humela* is the Latinised form of the old German for hops. The Latin word *humus* means ground, *lupus* means wolf because of the hook like teeth that help the plant climb, strangling their victims and 'hoppen' is the old name for hops
FAMILY:	**Cannabaceae**
EDIBLE PART:	Young shoots (for the fruits see September 16th)
EDIBILITY RATING:	3
WHERE IT'S FOUND:	Hedgerow, woodland edge, dappled to full sun
CAUTIONS:	Avoid during pregnancy as it has an antispasmodic effect on the uterus. It can cause dermatitis for some people and avoid if you have cancers of the breast, uterus or cervix. Avoid if you have depression as it can have a sedative effect
LOOKALIKES	Other climbers can become entwined with hops, so make sure you are picking just hops! Other climbers could be black bryony *Tamus communis* which is toxic (with heart shaped shiny leaves and strings of berries) or bindweed *Calystegia sepium* (also heart shaped floppy leaves and trumpet-like white flowers) which doesn't agree with everyone
MONTH SPAN:	(hz 5) flowers July - August, seeds ripen September - October, in leaf from May

| FOOD IDEAS: | Hop shoots are so delicious fried as a snack or in an omelette but put loads in so you can get the full flavour |
| RECIPE: | I know this is so simple but I think it rivals popcorn as a delicious snack! Pick as many hop shoots as you can, by pinching off the long tips. Melt butter in a frying pan and once melted, add the hop shoots. If using salted butter, you probably won't need any additional salt. When turning golden and crispy, tip into a bowl and pick out your favourite movie! If you want to make hop shoot omelette, use plenty of hop shoots to appreciate their full hoppy flavour |

" I SAID A HIP HIP THE HIPPIE THE HIPPIE TO THE HIPHIP HOP, AND YOU DON'T STOP THE ROCK IT TO THE BANG BANG BOOGIE"

Sugarhill Gang, Rappers delight

ALKANET

Anchusa officinalis

NAME ORIGIN:	The Greek word *anchousa* means a cosmetic paint for staining the skin and *officinalis* means of the apothecary's shop suggesting it is used medicinally
FAMILY:	Boraginaceae

EDIBLE PART:	Flowers, leaves, young shoots
EDIBILITY RATING:	2
WHERE IT'S FOUND:	Waste ground, pastures, roadsides
CAUTIONS:	None known although plants in this family if eaten in large quantities can have a damaging effect on the liver
MONTH SPAN:	Flowers June - October (hz 5)

FOOD IDEAS	Cook the young shoots and leaves as a vegetable, flowers cooked or eaten raw, use as a garnish on salads, etc.
OTHER INFO:	The roots produce an edible red dye

SPIDER CRAB
Maja squinado

NAME ORIGIN:	*Maia* is Greek for the mother of Mercury and the month of May is dedicated to her. *Squinado* means angular.
FAMILY:	Majidae

EDIBLE PART:	Meat.
EDIBILITY RATING:	5
WHERE IT'S FOUND:	Rocky shores, plenty of seaweed
CAUTIONS:	Avoid if allergic to shellfish. Ask advice from your doctor before eating if you are pregnant
MONTH SPAN:	Spring is best, into summer

FOOD IDEAS:	Cook for 20 minutes per kilo, boil, take your time extracting the meat and eat as it is, or with a little melted butter. If you have a fair bit of meat, then make crab mousse, crab linguine, crab and chilli on toast, anything crabby that you fancy!
OTHER INFO:	Antoine, Flo, Nick and I went camping near Polzeath many years ago. We took our spear guns and snorkels and it was Antoine who came up trumps with our dinner! He had speared one spider crab and had handpicked another, bringing them to the surface for us to boil up. Amazing! The meat on them is so delicious. Try and pick the ones with the knackered crusty old shell as these are the best to eat. The females must have 120mm minimum width of carapace and males with a minimum of 130mm.

SPIDER CRAB LINGUINE

Serves 4

400g linguine
1 tbsp extra virgin olive oil plus extra for drizzling
2 garlic cloves
1 red chilli
a splash of white wine
1 lemon
200g spider crab white crabmeat
Small bunch of flat-leaf parsley
seasoning
Extra virgin olive oil, to finish

Cook the linguine in a large pan of boiling salted water and drain in a colander. Peel the garlic and finely chop along with the chilli (deseed if you wish) and pan fry in the olive oil on a gentle heat until softened. Add the zest of half the lemon, the juice of the whole lemon and a splash of wine, then add the cooked linguine and the white crabmeat, tossing it to combine. Roughly chop the flat-leaf parsley, sprinkle it over the pasta then drizzle with the extra oil. Season to taste.

OTHER INFO:

Liquorice roots contain a substance called glycyrrhizin which is 30 - 50 times sweeter than sucrose. The first time I tried liquorice sticks was in Switzerland when we were staying in Beatenberg, situated above Lake Thun, with breath-taking views of the 3 mountains called Eiger, Mönch and Jungfrau (the ogre, the monk and the maiden). I felt like 'Heidi' as the chalet we stayed in had a sleeping mezzanine which was like a hayloft! Chewing liquorice sticks (roots) can be messy as they are very fibrous but surprisingly are good for your teeth and act like a tooth-cleaner. The majority of liquorice is grown commercially as a flavouring for the tobacco industry. It is found in beauty products to reduce the appearance of age spots.

LIQUORICE

Glycyrrhiza glabra

SYNONYM:	*Glycyrrhiza glandulifera, Glycyrrhiza pallida, Glycyrrhiza hirsuta, Glycyrrhiza violacea*
NAME ORIGIN:	*Glycyrrhiza* comes from the Greek *glukus* meaning sweet and *rhiza* meaning root. *Glabra* means smooth.
FAMILY:	**Fabaceae**
EDIBLE PART:	Roots and leaves
EDIBILITY RATING:	5
WHERE IT'S FOUND:	Sunny position, sandy soil, can be found near the coast.
CAUTIONS:	Use with caution during pregnancy, avoid consuming too much as it can cause high blood pressure, oedema and congestive heart failure!
LOOKALIKES:	Other leguminous trees look similar but liquorice is a herbaceous perennial and has pinnate leaves with 9 to 17 leaflets.
MONTH SPAN:	Flowers June – July, (hz 8)

FOOD IDEAS:	Use the leaves to make a thirst-quenching tea, the roots are used as a flavouring, either by simmering in water and using that liquid, or by extracting powder from the roots. You can also infuse the roots in milk or cream to use for ice creams, panna cottas, etc. Try it to make sweets, a sauce to go with salmon or other fish… it goes well with strong flavours such as ginger and mint as well as rhubarb and raspberries.

COMMON BROOM scotch broom
Cytisus scoparius

SYNONYM:	*Sarothamnus scoparius, Spartium scoparium, Sarothamnus vulgaris, Sarothamnus bourgaei*
NAME ORIGIN:	*Kytisos* is Greek for trefoil referring to the leaves of many species and the Latin word *scopae* means a broom. Many *Cytisus* species come from Cythnos, an island in the Aegean.
FAMILY:	Fabaceae
EDIBLE PART:	Flowers
EDIBILITY RATING:	2
WHERE IT'S FOUND:	Coastal, pastures, heathland
CAUTION:	Avoid during pregnancy and eat in moderation – caution is advised. The plant depresses respiration, hearing and effects the heart function. Avoid if you have high blood pressure
LOOKALIKES:	Spanish broom *Spartium junceum* has poisonous flowers so don't muddle them up!
MONTH SPAN:	Flowers May - June, seeds ripen August – November

FOOD IDEAS:	Pickle flower buds or add to salads
OTHER INFO:	This plant is called broom along with other names such as besom as it was often used to make brooms. It is a useful plant for stabilising sand dunes and the 'thatch' you get from it makes excellent screening, thatching for roofs and is used in basketry.

SEA ARROWGRASS
Triglochin maritima

NAME ORIGIN:	*Triglochin* possibly means 3 spikes, *maritima* means coastal/from the sea
FAMILY:	**Juncinaceae**
EDIBLE PART:	Base of the leaves, the unripe seeds
EDIBILITY RATING:	4
WHERE IT'S FOUND:	Estuaries, marshes, shoreline
CAUTIONS:	Toxic to grazing cattle and sheep, due to cyanogenic glycosides. Avoid picking in dog walking areas
LOOKALIKES:	*Plantago maritima* sea plantain looks similar but the leaves of sea plantain have fine ribs running the length of the leaves and the seeds are more spaced out on the flower spike. Sea plantain is edible and doesn't taste like salty coriander
MONTH SPAN:	Mostly all year round but dies back slightly in the winter

FOOD IDEAS:	Finely chop the base of the leaves for a coriander flavour in dishes – good for fish tacos, vinaigrettes, rice dishes, etc. Use the unripe seeds the same way or for a coriander favoured garnish
OTHER INFO:	Sea arrowgrass is really delicious and worth trying if you haven't before. As mentioned in cautions, as the leaves grow, the darker green parts begin to develop hydrocyanic acid which can affect your body's oxygen uptake but the pale bases, young flower shoots and seeds are safe to eat

NIPPLEWORT dock cress
Lapsana communis

NAME ORIGIN:	**It is called nipplewort because the closed flower buds resemble nipples. It has been used to treat sore nipples during breast-feeding and has been used in trials to help with breast tumours.** *Lapsana* **is Latin for charlock and** *communis* **means community/growing in company, as they self-seed well and create carpets of the plants.**
FAMILY:	**Asteraceae**
EDIBLE PART:	Leaves and young shoots
EDIBILITY RATING:	2
WHERE IT'S FOUND:	Garden weed, roadsides, waste ground, any aspect, woodland edges, hedgerows
MONTH SPAN:	Flowers June - September, seeds ripen August - October (hz 5)

FOOD IDEAS:	Eat leaves raw or cooked, can be added to soups and savoury dishes. As with most leaves, pick before the plant flowers as they can become bitter. Young leaves are good raw and the more hairy older ones are best cooked.
OTHER INFO:	Nipplewort has been used to make a tea which helps stop milk flow when you are stopping breastfeeding. Eating the leaves is meant to give a calming effect.

HEARTSEASE
Viola tricolor

NAME ORIGIN:	*Tricolor* means 3 colours as the flowers are made of 3 colours. The name 'heartsease' refers to its supposed powers of healing a broken heart. *Viola* is the Ancient Latin name for a violet.
FAMILY:	**Violaceae**

EDIBLE PART:	Flowers, flower buds, young leaves
EDIBILITY RATING:	3
WHERE IT'S FOUND:	Cultivated ground, meadows, lawns, grassland
MONTH SPAN:	Flowers April - September, seeds ripen June - September (hz 4)

FOOD IDEAS:	Young leaves and flowers can be used to garnish food or add to salads, all parts can be used to thicken soups, use raw or cooked
OTHER INFO:	Heartsease is technically a pansy and the word comes from the French pensées meaning thoughts as this flower is associated with love. Used in love potions, according to Roman mythology, Cupid shot an arrow and it struck this plant, therefore giving it the ability to act as a love potion.

WHITEBAIT

Clupea sp.

NAME ORIGIN:	***Clupea* means anchovy in Latin. Other fish in this order include herring, sprats and anchovies**
FAMILY:	**Clupeidae**

EDIBLE PART:	Meat - the whole thing!
EDIBILITY RATING:	5
WHERE IT'S FOUND:	Sea, estuaries and occasionally rivers
CAUTIONS:	None known but avoid if you are allergic to fish
MONTH SPAN:	April – September

FOOD IDEAS:	Eat whitebait lightly coated in seasoned flour and deep fried, served with lemon and aioli
OTHER INFO:	I like to play with my food; whitebait is one of my favourites!! Whitebait in breadcrumbs with its head dipped in tartare sauce, mayo or aioli suddenly turns into a fishy catwalk of different coiffured beauties and the game becomes 'who is the fishy celebrity that you are about to bite the head off'. It is very tasty and I promise not as sadistic as it sounds... just a lot of yummy fishy fun! Whitebait can be many different species of immature fish, but in the UK, it mostly refers to herring. Remember that by eating juvenile fish in large quantities it can reduce fish stocks so catch only what you can eat.

SAND EELS

Ammodytes tobianus **lesser sand eel**
Hyperoplus lanceolatus **greater sand eel**

NAME ORIGIN:	*Ammodytes* comes from the Greek *'ammos'* meaning sand and *'dutes'* meaning burrower or diver
FAMILY:	Ammodytidae
EDIBLE PART:	Whole thing
EDIBILITY RATING:	4
WHERE IT'S FOUND:	In the sea, swimming near the sea bed, buried in wet sand
MONTH SPAN:	April - September

FOOD IDEAS:	Sand eels can be eaten like white bait. Remove the head and gut them, then either grill them or coat in breadcrumbs and fry
OTHER INFO:	These aren't actually eels but a type of fish and are a very important food source to a lot of marine life, including puffins, gannets, seals, dolphins and fledgling seabirds. Unfortunately, they have at times been over-fished for the food industry and other industries which has had a major knock-on effect on sea bird populations in particular. If you decide to eat these, please only collect a few for your own consumption

Sand eels are used for fishing as they are naturally eaten by so many different species, including bass and mackerel |

WATER HAWTHORN STEW (SOUTH AFRICAN RECIPE)
Serves 2

sunflower oil for frying
500g lamb short ribs
1 onion
1 tbsp brown sugar
1 tsp sea salt
1 tsp freshly ground black pepper
1 tsp paprika
1/4 tsp garlic powder
1/4 tsp onion powder
250ml boiling water
300g water hawthorn flowers
2 potatoes, peeled and cubed
Juice of ½ a lemon

Heat the sunflower oil in a large saucepan and brown the meat. Remove the meat and put to one side. Peel and chop the onion, adding it to the meat oil and cooking until translucent, then add the meat back in with the brown sugar, sea salt, black pepper, paprika, garlic and onion powder. Cook for a minute, then add the water and simmer on a low heat until the lamb is tender. Add the potatoes and water hawthorn and simmer until the potato is cooked and starting to fall apart. Serve with lemon juice (and season to taste).

WATER HAWTHORN

Aponogeton distachyos

NAME ORIGIN:	**The word *apon* is Celtic for water, *geiton* means neighbour and *distachyos* means 2 spiked. The plant spreads in ponds hence 'water neighbour' and the flower is 'two-spiked'**
FAMILY:	**Aponogetonaceae**

EDIBLE PART:	Flowers, tubers, flowering stem, leaves
EDIBILITY RATING:	3
WHERE IT'S FOUND:	Ponds, lakes
MONTH SPAN:	Flowers April - October (hz 9)

FOOD IDEAS:	Eat the raw flowers as they are delicious and crunchy. Roast the tuber, the flowering spike can be cooked or eaten raw like spinach and eat the stem like an asparagus substitute.
OTHER INFO:	The first time I saw this was at one of my favourite places - Coleton Fishacre. This place is an incredible National Trust house which belonged to the D'Oyly Carte family who were behind the operettas of Gilbert and Sullivan, as well as developing the Savoy Hotel and Claridges. If you like art deco style, you must visit this house. Water hawthorn is a beautiful plant, and to find out it was edible too, was fantastic! Sweet, crunchy and delicious.... and its white blooms make it great for a black and white dinner party (black squid ink pasta, sushi, etc.)! In South Africa, the plant is commonly eaten and referred to, in Afrikaans, as "waterblommetjies", meaning "little water flowers" as well as "Wateruintje" meaning "water onion".

RAMANAS ROSE; DOG ROSE

Rosa rugosa; Rosa canina

SYNONYM:	*Rosa ferox*; no synonym
NAME ORIGIN:	*Rosa* is the Latin word for rose, *rugosa* means wrinkled and *canina* comes from the Latin *canis* meaning dog
FAMILY:	**Rosaceae**
EDIBLE PART:	Flowers, leaves (see cautions) (young shoots in spring, hips in autumn)
EDIBILITY RATING:	4
WHERE IT'S FOUND:	*Rosa rugosa* – sandy beaches, dunes, sea shores, hedging *Rosa canina* – hedges, dappled shade, woodland
OTHER DATE:	See October 2nd
CAUTIONS:	Hydrogen cyanide is in the leaves and seeds, but not in the flowers or fruit. Small doses are fine. The hairs on seeds can irritate.

MONTH SPAN:	*Rosa rugosa* – flowers June – August, fruit/seeds ripen August – October *Rosa canina* – flowers June – July, seeds ripen October – December hz 3
FOOD IDEAS:	Eat the petals, add them to salads, use them to make Turkish delight with heavily scented ones, rose petal syrup, rose petal jam, crystallised petals, dry the petals and make your own ras-el-hanout spice mix. A very simple yet delicious way of preparing them is rose petal preserve – whizz up rose petals, lemon juice and caster sugar and use it to spread on sponge cakes, stir into yoghurt served with mango… the flavour and colour is fantastic, especially when using Ramanas rose.

ROSE PETAL JELLY

Serves 2

I ltr heavily scented
pink rose petals
I kg jam sugar
(can use normal sugar)
2 lemons

Use a litre measuring jug and pick off the most open undamaged blossoms (just the petals not the whole flower) and fill it, checking for pests. In a saucepan put the petals and Iltr water together and bring to the boil. Simmer for 15 minutes, strain through a sieve and leave the liquid to cool and infuse.

Juice the 2 lemons and add the juice to the cooled rose water, add the sugar and return to the heat on medium temperature. Stir until dissolved then turn up the heat until it reaches a rolling boil (this will take about 10 minutes). Test by dropping a little on a chilled plate and when you push it with your finger it should wrinkle up which means it is ready. Put it in sterilised jars and store or eat!

OTHER INFO:

Rosa rugosa flowers harness free radicals as they are full of anti-oxidants and so are used in cosmetics for their anti-ageing properties. The flowers have been tested at varying stages of development and the most potent stage is the first, when the buds are just forming.

FAIRY RING CHAMPIGNON
Marasmius oreades

NAME ORIGIN:	The name *Marasmius* comes from a Greek word *marasmus* which means to dry out. The species *oreades* means mountain nymph from Middle English and both Latin and Greek have similar words – *oros* means mountain
FAMILY:	**Marasmiaceae**

EDIBLE PART:	Mushroom
EDIBILITY RATING:	3
WHERE IT'S FOUND:	Lawns, pastures, short grass
CAUTIONS:	These must be cooked as they contain hydrogen cyanide
LOOKALIKES:	Fool's funnel *Clitocybe rivulosa* which could cause a fatal mistake. The main difference is that fool's funnel has a pale crust on the cap. Don't assume that because it is in a ring formation that it is automatically fairy ring champignon. There are about 50 species that grow like this including *Scleroderma, Agaricus* and *Lycoperdon*

MONTH SPAN:	Spring – autumn
FOOD IDEAS:	The stems are too tough to eat so remove and just cook the caps; they can be pickled and preserved in oil. They go well with rich meats
OTHER INFO:	Fairy ring champignons often grow in rings, because they are growing on organic material such as old tree stumps, logs, roots, etc. and the mycelium radiates outwards producing a ring formation. The hydrogen cyanide that they produce damages the epidermal cells and root hairs of grass, allowing the fungus to push up more easily through it
	There is much folklore about fairy rings – enter at your peril! The hazards of entering a ring are you may become invisible, trapped in the fairy realm never able to escape, you could lose an eye or be forced to dance around the ring forever until you go mad or die of exhaustion!

FAIRY RING CHAMPIGNON AND BACON ON TOAST

Serves 2

Butter and oil (to fry in and spread on toast)
4 pieces of sliced bread
2 large handfuls of fairy ring champignon caps
4 rashers of bacon
juice of half a lemon
1 handful of flat leaf parsley
a splash of white wine
seasoning

In a frying pan, dry fry the bacon rashers on both sides until golden. Remove the rashers and put to one side. Add butter and oil to fry in the pan, and when sizzling, add the mushroom caps and toss well, turning until golden. (Toast the bread now). When they have good colour, add the lemon juice, wine and seasoning and allow to simmer until most of the liquid has been absorbed and evaporated. Butter the toast and top with the bacon rashers and mushrooms. Chop the parsley roughly and sprinkle over and serve.

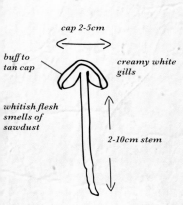

cap 2-5cm

buff to
tan cap

creamy white
gills

whitish flesh
smells of
sawdust

2-10cm stem

fairy ring champignon

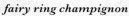

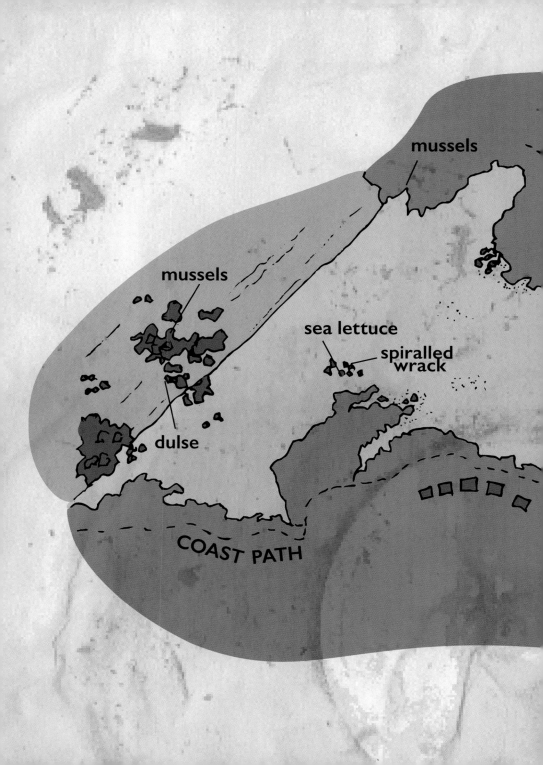

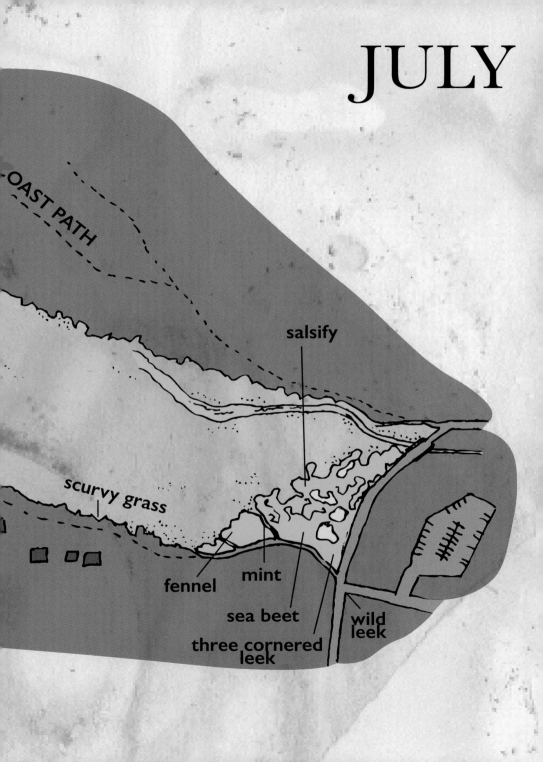

JULY

COAST PATH

salsify

scurvy grass

fennel

mint

sea beet

three cornered
leek

wild
leek

WILD BASIL
Clinopodium vulgare

SYNONYM:	*Calamintha clinopodium, Calamintha vulgaris*
NAME ORIGIN:	The name originates from the Greek *klino* meaning a 'bed', *podion* means 'a little foot' and *vulgare* means 'common'
FAMILY:	Lamiaceae

EDIBLE PART:	Leaves
EDIBILITY RATING:	3
WHERE IT'S FOUND:	Grassland, heathland
CAUTIONS:	None known
LOOKALIKES:	The leaves look a bit like oregano
MONTH SPAN:	Flowers June - September, seeds ripen August – September

FOOD IDEAS:	Dried or fresh leaves are good in salads, as a tea or used as a flavouring
OTHER INFO:	Wild basil is good as a tea for aiding digestion and stimulating the appetite

ROASTED TOMATO TART WITH WILD BASIL SORBET

For the basil sorbet
3 1/2 oz caster sugar
7 fl oz water
2 good handfuls wild basil leaves and stem
1/2 lemon

In a saucepan put the water and sugar together. Simmer until the sugar has dissolved, then add the basil and simmer together for 5 minutes. Take off the heat and leave to cool and infuse. Add the juice of half a lemon when cool. Put in an ice cream maker or freeze for a couple of hours, mash up with a fork, return to the freezer and repeat.

For the tomato tart
1 lb cherry tomatoes
3 fl oz balsamic vinegar
8 oz puff pastry
1 tbsp caster sugar
2 tbsp wild basil or thyme

Preheat the oven to 190 degrees C
In an oven proof frying pan heat gently the sugar, balsamic and thyme or wild basil until the sugar is dissolved. Mix together with a wooden spoon, then add the cherry tomatoes so they fill the pan. Roll out the puff pastry and drape it over the tomatoes. Take off the heat and pop in the oven for about 1/2 an hour or until the pastry has risen and is golden. When cooked, leave to cool slightly. Put a plate face down on the pan, then using oven gloves flip over so the tomatoes are on top. Serve with the sorbet and a dollop of crème fraiche if you wish. Season accordingly.

EVENING PRIMROSE
Oenothera biennis

SYNONYM:	*Onagra biennis, Onagra muricata, Oenothera muricata, Brunyera biennis*
NAME ORIGIN:	The name comes from the Greek *oinos* meaning wine and *thera* meaning to pursue or imbibe. The meaning behind this is unclear but it could be due to a certain species of *Oenothera* which induces a taste for wine. In Latin, *oenothera* means a plant whose juice may cause sleep. *Biennis* means biennial. *Onagra* means asses food - another suggestion is *oenothera* may be a corruption of the Greek *onotheras* from *onos* for ass and *thera* for hunting(!).
FAMILY:	**Onagraceae**
EDIBLE PART:	Flowers, seeds, roots
EDIBILITY RATING:	3
WHERE IT'S FOUND:	Waste ground, roadsides, dunes, sandy soil
CAUTIONS:	Avoid if you are on anticoagulants or on phenothiazines (allergy antihistamines) as evening primrose can trigger seizures. Avoid if you are prone to epileptic fits. It can cause headaches, diarrhoea and nausea.
MONTH SPAN:	Flowers from June - September, seeds ripen July - October (hz4)

FOOD IDEAS:	Flowers in salads and the ripe seeds are a good source of GLA (gamma-linolenic acid). The roots can be cooked and eaten – they taste weirdly of chicken and can make you cough a bit as they are slightly irritant! The roots are at their best when harvested in autumn.
OTHER INFO:	Evening primrose oil which is extracted from the seeds is fantastic for skin conditions such as eczema, acne plus other skin complaints and also for rheumatoid arthritis and pre-menstrual syndrome (PMS).

WILD STRAWBERRY
Fragaria vesca

NAME ORIGIN:	*Fraga* is Latin for strawberry, *vesca* means small and feeble (puny).
FAMILY:	**Rosaceae**

EDIBLE PART:	Fruits, leaves
EDIBILITY RATING:	5
WHERE IT'S FOUND:	Partial to full shade, damp soil, woodland
CAUTIONS:	Babies can be allergic to strawberries so be aware when you are weaning them.
LOOKALIKES:	Barren strawberry *Potentilla sterilis*. The main difference is that this doesn't produce delicious fruits! The petals of the barren strawberry are separated by wide gaps, it flowers March - June which is earlier than wild strawberries and the point on the end of the leaflet (terminal tooth) is shorter than the points (teeth) on either side of it, while wild strawberries have a longer point jutting out further than those on either side. *Potentilla indica/Duchesnea indica* is known as the mock strawberry or Indian strawberry. The flowers are yellow not white and the calyx flairs back away from the fruit – tasteless but non-toxic although they can cause allergic reactions.
MONTH SPAN:	Flowers April - May, fruits June – September

FOOD IDEAS:	Wild strawberry jam, Eton mess if you can pick enough – a good tip is you can freeze them until you get enough. Coulis, wild strawberry ice cream with black pepper shortbread. The leaves can be dried to make a delicious tea that has a slight mint-like taste to it. Dry the fruits to use at a later date.

WILD STRAWBERRY JAM (1 JAR)

250g wild strawberries
40g jam sugar
1/2 lemon

Put a small plate in the fridge to chill it so you can check the jam is set later on. Put the strawberries, sugar and squeeze the lemon in to a saucepan and heat gently to a simmer.

Stir to melt the sugar and prevent sticking and check a small dollop of the jam on the cold plate after 5 minutes - this is a really quick jam to make and so delicious.

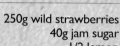

OTHER INFO:

The pips are tiny nutlets which are a good source of dietary fibre. When I was about 13, Mum, Dad, my mate Lisa and myself decided to cycle the Camel Trail from Wadebridge to Padstow as it was such a glorious summer. Mum and Dad managed to accumulate bikes fairly easily and borrowed Grandad and Nana Joan's collapsible bikes for Lisa and I. I had Grandad's bike and every 5 minutes, the seat would jerk itself skyward, flipping me back into a hunchback stance, so much so that I couldn't take it anymore and had to stop for a little pity cry (I was 13 remember, so acceptable behaviour, it's not like I do this all the time...). One of the times I stopped was near the slate piles and as far as the eye could see were wild strawberries. If you ever have a pity cry, the sight of ripe delicious red jewels certainly helps return you from the brink of despair that your Grandad's collapsible bike might push you to.

Did you know you can use the roots to whiten teeth and were once used to bleach freckles?

OTHER INFO:

My Great Granny would ask Dad and his brothers to go and pick sampeth, which was marsh samphire. I foraged for it in the same place with Dad and it is so delicious. Don't get muddled up with rock samphire which is in the carrot family and grows out of cliffs, rocky areas or even walls. People used to lose their lives trying to harvest it from cliffs to pickle or eat steamed as a vegetable. Marsh samphire is like a skinny succulent, made of segments that grows in muddy estuaries which is a little less dangerous a plant to capture (even though rock samphire grows in abundance in easy to reach places!) You can eat it raw, or steam it gently and serve it with a little butter, delicious with fish. It is naturally salty. As it gets older, it develops a 'spine' in the middle where it becomes woody. When it is like this, it is still fine to eat, but you need to scrape it off the woody centre with your teeth - well worth it! The common name 'glasswort' is so called because the soda ash from the burnt plant was used in the glass making industry (sodium carbonate). When you go picking samphire, please try and remember to take scissors as this is the best way of harvesting without uprooting the plant.

SMOKED TROUT AND SAMPHIRE LINGUINE

Serves 2

175g linguine
250g marsh samphire, rinsed (and any strands of seaweed removed)
250g smoked trout, cut into bite-sized pieces (2cmsq)
1/2 lemon
A knob of butter
Olive oil
black pepper

In a saucepan bring water to the boil, drizzle a little oil in and cook the linguine until al dente (about 10 minutes). For the last 2 minutes drop the samphire in to the boiling water with the linguine. In a frying pan, melt the butter and pan fry the smoked trout until no longer opaque. Add the zest of the lemon, drain the pasta and samphire and add to the frying pan. Squeeze the juice of the lemon over, add the black pepper then toss to completely combine. Drizzle with a little oil and serve. If you like a bit of a kick, then sprinkle over a small pinch of chilli flakes.

MARSH SAMPHIRE

Glasswort

Salicornia europaea

SYNONYMS:	*Salicornia herbacea*
NAME ORIGIN:	*Europaea* means European, the Celtic word *sal* means near and *lis* means water
FAMILY:	Chenopodiaceae

EDIBLE PART:	Aerial parts
EDIBILITY RATING:	5
WHERE IT'S FOUND:	Coastal areas, mud and salt flats, estuaries
CAUTIONS:	Pick from a clean area, especially in dog walking areas. Make sure the water quality is good in the area – you can check water quality on the internet.
MONTH SPAN:	April/May – September

FOOD IDEAS:	Eat it raw or steam for 5 mins and serve as a vegetable, as a bed of 'sea vegetables' with pan fried smoked haddock with crispy skin (and a homemade hollandaise?). Excellent in a flan or quiche, raw in salad, blitzed into a sauce. Try doing them in a tempura batter.

WILD CHERRY
Prunus avium

SYNONYM	*Cerasus nigra, Cerasus sylvestris*
NAME ORIGIN:	*Prunus* is the classical name for plum and *avis* is Latin for bird. The tree possibly originated from a place called Cerasunt, a Greek city in the country of the Colchians.
FAMILY:	Rosaceae

EDIBLE PART:	Fruits
EDIBILITY RATING:	4
WHERE IT'S FOUND:	Hedgerow, deciduous woodland
CAUTIONS:	The leaves and seed contain hydrogen cyanide, so don't eat! Okay in small quantities, but the ripe fruit is the best bit anyway!
LOOKALIKES:	Sour cherry *Prunus cerasus*, bird cherry *Prunus padus* and cherry plum *Prunus cerasifera* look similar and none are poisonous. The fruits of wild cherry have longer stalks than sour cherry, bird cherry have black fruit and plum cherry are larger and red. Wild cherry has beautiful bark which is red/maroon and glossy.
MONTH SPAN:	Flowers from April - May, fruits ripen from late June – August

FOOD IDEAS:	Cherry clafoutis, cherry brandy, cherry jam, cherry leather
RECIPE:	Stewed cherries are easy to make and can be added to alcohol, cakes, turned in to jam, served with ice cream or yoghurt. However many cherries you've got, remove the stone, put in a saucepan with a little water and simmer. Add sugar to taste but mind you don't burn your mouth whilst testing!

OTHER INFO: Speed and a keen eye are essential for beating squirrels and birds to this prize fruit! Get to know what the leaves look like in June, and whenever you are on a walk, if you spot a tree, take your time thoroughly looking over every reachable part for the green unripe dangling fruit. Every time you do this same walk, stop and check for ripeness. Cherries have a fairly short picking period, but very worth it. Cherries can vary from sweet to sour so chose your recipe accordingly. In the spring, I love collecting cherry blossom buds and making preserved cherry blossom, aka Sakura. They have incredible flavour – salty, sweet, sour, fruity.

ELDERFLOWER CORDIAL

12 flower heads
2 cups sugar
2 tsp citric acid
2 lemons
750ml water

Shake the elderflower heads to remove any insects and put the flowers in a large bowl - I keep the flower head whole but cut off as much stem as possible. Peel or zest the lemons and slice the remaining lemons pith and all, putting all of it in the same bowl. In a saucepan heat the water and sugar until the sugar has dissolved and the water is just simmering. Pour over the elderflower and lemon, then sprinkle the citric acid on top. Cover with cling film and leave overnight. Strain keeping the liquid, squeezing the elderflower heads to get as much liquid as possible. Bottle or dilute and serve.

OTHER INFO:

Dad and I made elderflower cordial for the first time when I was about 12. We'd found a decent sized plant, laden with aromatic creamy flower clusters in Rosudgeon (near Penzance) so we picked enough and returned home to make the cordial. The recipe we use means waiting 24 hours while the mixture steeps - 24 hours for a 12 year old is such a long time!!!! Well worth it though as I can still remember how good it was!
Elder has been found in Neolithic graves, used for food and medicine for at least 4000 years.

ELDERFLOWER

Sambucus nigra

SYNONYM:	*Sambucus graveolens, Sambucus peruviana*
NAME ORIGIN:	*Aeld* is the Anglo-Saxon word for fire as the hollow elder stems were used to blow on a fire to increase the heat for blacksmithing. *Sambucus* comes from the Ancient Latin name for elder and *nigra* means black, referring to the black berries. *Sambuca* is the Latin name of the harp-like musical instrument made from elder.
FAMILY:	Adoxaceae
EDIBLE PART:	Flower (corymbs)
EDIBILITY RATING:	5
WHERE IT'S FOUND:	Roadsides, hedgerow, waste ground, woodland edge, coastal (everywhere!)
OTHER DATES:	For the berries see September 7th
CAUTIONS:	Almost all parts of the plant except the fruit and the flowers contain a cyanide-inducing glycoside. The seeds do too, but in small quantities. At the most it will cause slight stomach upset. The fruit can be eaten raw - spit out the pips or cooking the fruit is best.
LOOKALIKES:	The creamy white umbels of many plants in the carrot family (Apiaceae) look similar to the creamy corymbs of elder BUT elder is a tree or shrub so the size is a big giveaway. *Viburnum opulus* guelder rose has similar creamy flowers but without the typical elderflower scent and elder corymbs are flat.
MONTH SPAN:	Flowers June - July
FOOD IDEAS:	Eat the flowers raw or stew them with fruits, in jams, pies, etc. Make wine, champagne or cordial - you can freeze the cordial in a plastic bottle to make it last. Well worth trying elderflower ice cream too (infuse the flowers in the cream to extract the flavour). There is a fantastic recipe for elderflower delight - like Turkish delight, in the River Cottage Hedgerow handbook which is incredible, well worth trying.

RED VALERIAN
Centranthus ruber

NAME ORIGIN:	*Ruber* means red, The Greek word *kentron* means a spur and *anthos* means a flower
FAMILY:	**Valerianaceae**

EDIBLE PART:	Young leaves, roots
EDIBILITY RATING:	1
WHERE IT'S FOUND:	Coastal, walls, waste ground
CAUTIONS:	None known
MONTH SPAN:	Flowers June - August, seeds ripen July – September

FOOD IDEAS:	Eat the young leaves either raw or cooked (quite bitter). Cook the roots and try as a vegetable or add to a soup.
OTHER INFO:	Red valerian and valerian are often confused by their common names but they are completely different plants - the roots of valerian (true valerian is *Valeriana officinalis*) are used as a sedative and were supposedly used by the Pied Piper of Hamlyn to coax away the rats by sewing it into his cloak as they love the smell. Red valerian does not possess these properties.

LINDEN, LIME

Tilia cordata small leaved lime
Tilia x *europaea* common lime

SYNONYM:	For *Tilia cordata* – *Tilia microphylla, Tilia parvifolia, Tilia ulmifolia* For *Tilia* x *europaea* – *Tilia officinarum, Tilia intermedia*
NAME ORIGIN:	*Tilia* comes from the Greek *ptilon* meaning wing as the flowers have a wing-like bract. The species *cordata* means heart shaped and the other species name means from Europe. The old English name was linde which gives us the name linden.
FAMILY:	**Tiliaceae** or **Malvaceae**
EDIBLE PART:	**Leaves, flowers**
EDIBILITY RATING:	3
WHERE IT'S FOUND:	Broadleaf woodland
CAUTIONS:	If you are making tea from the old flowers, it can cause a narcotic intoxication
LOOKALIKES:	Not a lookalike but the common name lime has nothing to do with the citrus fruit
MONTH SPAN:	Flowers June - July, young leaves available from spring to autumn, seeds ripen in October
FOOD IDEAS:	A tea from the flowers is naturally sweet and calming. The young leaves are delicious raw in salads and are slightly mucilaginous. The flowers and immature fruit can be ground up, according to some, to produce a chocolate substitute, but I think it tastes more like vanilla, honey and parma violets - very delicious. The young leaves make a good sauce to go with seafood.
RECIPE:	Linden pudding - milky honey scented panna cotta Using carrageen to set, a little sugar and milk… Experiment with simmering plenty of linden flowers in milk and leaving to infuse for at least an hour, maybe even overnight! Then add sugar to taste, simmer carrageen in it, or use gelatine as instructed on the packet, until the mixture thickens. Pour into moulds and refrigerate.

Jute (*Corchorus capsularis*) is related to (in the same family) *Tilia*. The fragrant nectar filled flowers make an excellent medicinal honey – the sweet smell is due to an essential oil that contains farnesol which is also found in ylang ylang and jasmine. The wood has been used in the music industry for its good acoustic properties, to make things like guitar and bass bodies, drum shells and wind instruments, but these days it is more commonly used to make 'superstrat' types of guitars – if you've heard of basswood, then you are talking about *Tilia*.

DAYLILY

Hemerocallis sp. (fulva)

NAME ORIGIN:	**The Greek word *hemeros* means a day and *kallos* means beauty as the flowers last about a day.**
FAMILY:	**Hemerocallidaceae**
EDIBLE PART:	Flower buds, (young leaves), roots
EDIBILITY RATING:	3
WHERE IT'S FOUND:	Gardens, garden escape
CAUTIONS:	The only mention of toxins is that the leaves may cause hallucinations so best to avoid the leaves.
MONTH SPAN:	Flowers June - August (hz 4)

FOOD IDEAS:	Eat the flower buds raw or cooked, they can also act as a thickener in stews, soups, etc. The roots (tubers) can be eaten raw or cooked. Dig up the tubers, wash and toss in oil and sea salt before roasting. They taste very good, like a sweet potato flavour. They are quite small but you get quite a few without diminishing the plant too much (as they are clump-forming).
OTHER INFO:	The first time I tried this was when I was doing my work experience for Glyn at Erddig in North Wales. He opened my mind to many things including eating yew berries (not the green pip!!) and mowing in straight lines (not my strong point). There were daylilies growing and he got me to try them, when they were in bud. Quite pleasant to begin with, fantastic crisp texture, but after a while there is a lingering taste almost like alliums but not as nice and it can last for hours!

PUFFBALL BURGER

1 puffball (or a section of it)
2 eggs
2 slices brown bread
breadcrumbs
Sea salt
Oil or butter for frying
Granary baps
Pernod
Mayonnaise
Crunchy salad, tomatoes, blue cheese or strong cheddar for melting…

This is pretty straight forward! First of all stir a good splash of Pernod into a ½ cup of mayo until thoroughly combined – taste and add more or less mayo/Pernod. Slice up your puffball into 1cm thick slices and chop down to fit the granary baps. Crack the eggs into a bowl and beat with a fork then dip the puffball slices to coat them, then into the breadcrumbs. In a frying pan heat the oil or butter on a medium heat and fry the puffballs until golden on both sides. Season. Melt cheese on top of the puffball burger if you're using it, then construct your burger – crunchy salad, burger then a dollop of Pernod mayo.

7-80cm across

leathery,
white solid
and fleshy

giant puffball

GIANT PUFFBALL

Calvatia gigantea

SYNONYM:	*Langermannia gigantea*
NAME ORIGIN:	*Calvatia* comes from the Latin *calvaria* meaning dome of the skull and *gigantea* means gigantic.
FAMILY:	Lycoperdaceae

EDIBLE PART:	Mushroom
EDIBILITY RATING:	4
WHERE IT'S FOUND:	Grassland, pastures, gardens, occasionally woods
LOOKALIKES:	I have mistaken a bag of rubbish to be a giant puffball before, but no there isn't anything you could confuse a giant puffball for due to its size.
MONTH SPAN:	summer - autumn

FOOD IDEAS:	Soup, fried for breakfast or on toast, pâté, burger
OTHER INFO:	I had been told by quite a few people about the time they found a giant puffball and the rough whereabouts but never the exact location... My luck was in, finally, when I was talking to a neighbour of mine who gardens for people around the village. I was just on my way out to go foraging for ground elder, nettles, elderberries or anything else I could find and he happened to have spotted what must be a giant puffball on description. I couldn't believe it! He called the lady and asked if she was in, explained who I was and whether she minded me going to take a look. She agreed, I walked up to her house and sure enough, there in the hedge was my first ever giant puffball! One of the most disappointing things has to be when your eyes are attuned to spotting giant puffballs... you see one in the distance, you start salivating... as you get closer and closer you then realize... it's a lump of polystyrene or a plastic bag.... Argghhhh!!!

CHAMOMILE
Chamaemelum nobile

SYNONYM:	*Anthemis nobilis, Anthemis aurea.*
NAME ORIGIN:	*Anthemis* is the Greek name for chamomile and *nobile* means noble. The name chamomile means 'earth apple' due to the scent. It is also a flavouring in Spanish sherry, known as manzanilla, meaning 'little apples'.
FAMILY:	**Asteraceae**
EDIBLE PART:	Aerial parts - flowers and leaves
EDIBILITY RATING:	4
WHERE IT'S FOUND:	Sandy ground, roadsides, pasture
CAUTIONS:	Avoid if you have allergies to plants such as ragwort as it's in the same family
LOOKALIKES:	Mayweed *Anthemis cotula*, although the smell of this plant is not as pleasant. The juice of this plant can cause allergies.
MONTH SPAN:	Evergreen, flowers June - July
FOOD IDEAS:	The aerial parts especially the flowers are used as a flavouring, to make tea, to flavour milky puddings
OTHER INFO:	Chamomile tea is good for teething babies or children who can't (won't?) sleep. It is also very good for adults with anxiety and insomnia. Chamomile contains chamazulene, coumarins, heterosides and esters of angelic acid(!) which is rejuvenating and calming.

CHAMOMILE PANNA COTTA

A recipe from the Gourmet
traveller Magazine

30g gelatine (6 gelatine leaf
sheets)
1 ltr cream (pouring)
2 cups of milk
250g caster sugar
50g dried chamomile flowers
sugar thermometer

Soak the gelatine leaves in cold water for 5 minutes. Squeeze the gelatine sheets and put them in a large saucepan along with the cream, milk, chamomile flowers and sugar and heat gently until the temperature reaches 90 degrees C. Take off the heat, pour through a fine sieve into moulds lined with cling film and refrigerate. Cling film makes it easy to release the panna cotta from the moulds. Serve with mint leaves and homemade candied lemon rind.

ARTICHOKE; CARDOON

Cynara scolymus; Cynara cardunculus

NAME ORIGIN:	**The Greek word *kyon* means dog referring to teeth like spines, *scolymus* means globe artichoke and *cardunculus* means cardoon.**
FAMILY:	**Asteraceae**
EDIBLE PART:	Unripe flower base, base of sepals; the stem of cardoons
EDIBILITY RATING:	5
WHERE IT'S FOUND	Gardens, garden escape
CAUTIONS:	The sap can cause dermatitis on sensitive skin, may hinder lactation, use with caution if you suffer from a biliary obstruction
MONTH SPAN:	Flowers July - September

FOOD IDEAS:	Steamed or boiled globe artichokes with melted butter or a vinaigrette, the stems of cardoons peeled and boiled for 30-40 minutes until tender
OTHER INFO:	For globe artichokes pop them in boiling water, and when you can push a sharp knife in to the base (where the stem was) then they are ready. My favourite way which is perfect for a daydreamer who enjoys taking her time over pleasures such as this is to melt a load of salted butter, then working your way from the outside in, peel off the outer 'leaves' and dipping the base into the melted butter, scrape off the flesh with your teeth. Work your way in to the thinnest 'leaves', then once you are past that, you will reach the choke - the fluffy middle bit. Using a blunt knife, scrape the choke away to leave a disc-like middle attached to a little stem. Chop this in to cubes and put the whole lot in the melted butter, then savour very very slowwwwwly.

PELLITORY-OF-THE-WALL
Parietaria judaica

NAME ORIGIN:	*Parietaria* means wall-dweller in Latin and *judaica* means of Judaea/Jewish.
FAMILY:	**Urticaceae**

EDIBLE PART:	Leaves, aerial parts
EDIBILITY RATING:	3
WHERE IT'S FOUND:	Growing off the sides of buildings, stone walls, in hedges, cliffs
CAUTIONS:	The pollen is allergenic – if you are prone to allergies, treat with caution
MONTH SPAN:	Flowers from June to October

FOOD IDEAS:	Eat the leaves and tender aerial parts raw or cooked. They taste like cucumber and are delicious in salads and sandwiches.
OTHER INFO:	I've known of this plant for a long time but I didn't realize it was edible until I saw my dog Bramble eating it from the sides of buildings in St. Ives! This is a very common plant and once you recognize it, you'll start seeing it everywhere. Caterpillars of the Red Admiral butterfly eat it as their main food source.

3-7cm across

black brown,
warty

whitish
becoming
marbled
grey-brown

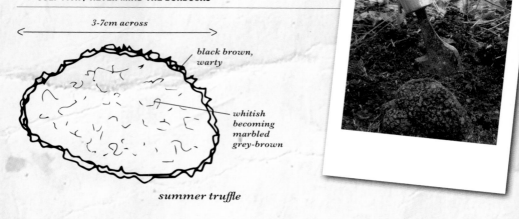

summer truffle

OTHER INFO:

Pigs were traditionally used to hunt for truffles but dogs are increasingly trained up these days to do the job, mostly because they will hunt but not eat and they are easier to transport. Truffles have a symbiotic relationship with the roots of suitable host species such as beech, oak and birch, but also holm oak, hazel, sycamore, hornbeam and hawthorn. There are 3 main types of truffle - black truffle, burgundy truffle (summer truffle) and white truffle - the latter being the most expensive. They can be the size of a marble up to the size of a golf ball (or more if you are really lucky!). A way of spotting a tree which may have truffles growing beneath it is if you notice any plants around the base of the tree look like they have been sprayed off or dying - the truffle removes competition for nutrients from other plants. Summer truffle and Burgundy truffle have been analysed and they are the same truffle but vary due to the conditions they are growing in.

SUMMER TRUFFLE; BURGUNDY TRUFFLE

Tuber aestivum; Tuber aestivum var. uncinatum

SYNONYM:	*Tuber uncinatum*
NAME ORIGIN:	*Aestivus* means summer and *tuber* means root/tuber. *Uncinatum* means hooked
FAMILY:	Tuberaceae
EDIBLE PART:	Tuber
EDIBILITY RATING:	4
WHERE IT'S FOUND:	Summer truffles prefer chalk and limestone soils, and the roots of beech, oak and birch
CAUTIONS:	None known
MONTH SPAN:	Harvest summer truffles from May – August, Burgundy truffles from September – January
FOOD IDEAS:	Infuse oil or use freshly shaved truffle on savoury dishes such as on pasta with pecorino or parmesan cheese, with eggs such as scrambled eggs, on pâté, with asparagus, scallops, crayfish, alliums such as garlic, leeks, onions and with cabbage.

PURPLE LOOSESTRIFE

Lythrum salicaria

NAME ORIGIN:	*Lythron* comes from the Greek for blood describing the colour of the leaves in autumn and *salicaria* means willow like.
FAMILY:	**Lythraceae**

EDIBLE PART:	Leaves, root
EDIBILITY RATING:	2
WHERE IT'S FOUND:	Damp ground, banks, marshland, marginal
CAUTIONS:	None known
LOOKALIKES:	The common name can be confused with other loosestrifes which are in the primula family Primulaceae. It looks similar to rosebay willowherb but purple loosestrife has opposite leaves where rosebay willowherb has whorls of leaves
MONTH SPAN:	Flowers June - August, seeds ripen August - September (hz 3)

FOOD IDEAS:	Cook the leaves and roots. The flowers can be used to produce an edible dye.
OTHER INFO:	This plant has been used to help treat diarrhoea in all ages, even in breast-feeding babies. The stems have been given to teething babies to strengthen their gums. This plant is classed as an invasive in some countries but with a healthy balance of insects that feed off this plant, it can be kept under control.

GOOSENECK BARNACLE

Common goose barnacle
Lepas anatifera

NAME ORIGIN:	**Their scientific name means bearer of ducklings. Geese were once believed to hatch from them!**
FAMILY:	*Lepadidae*
EDIBLE PART:	Meat inside the peduncle (neck-like part)
EDIBILITY RATING:	4
WHERE IT'S FOUND:	Growing on flotsam such as driftwood and plastic sea waste, growing on ships, seaweed and piers.
MONTH SPAN:	All year round, especially seen on beaches washed up after storms

FOOD IDEAS:	These can be cooked a number of ways, from boiling and squeezing them out of their sleeve (peduncle), sautéed with garlic (or ramsons), steamed in sea water or white wine and herbs and serve with pasta, with a creamy sherry sauce or olive oil, lemon and parsley.
RECIPE:	When cooking them, do not overcook – 1 minute boiled in sea water is all they need and squeeze them out of their peduncle when they are still warm. No need for a recipe but cook them like this then make your sauce of choice and toss them through for 30 seconds.
OTHER INFO:	Known as percebes, this is a well sought-after delicacy. The shellfish is made of 2 parts – the capitulum which has the feeding tentacles and the body called the peduncle which attaches to rocks or floating objects in the sea. Try and get them as fresh as possible because they can shrivel and dry out when out of water. These can grow on anything from driftwood, plastic and even creatures such as sea turtles!

DARWIN'S BARBERRY

Berberis darwinii

NAME ORIGIN:	*Berberis* comes from the Arabic name *berberys*. Charles Darwin discovered it in 1835 when voyaging on the 'Beagle'
FAMILY:	Berberidaceae
EDIBLE PART:	Flowers and fruit
EDIBILITY RATING:	3
WHERE IT'S FOUND:	Gardens, garden escape, shady woodland
CAUTIONS:	See other info
MONTH SPAN:	Flowers April - May, fruits July - August, hz 7

FOOD IDEAS:	Eat the fruit raw, cooked or dried when deseeded although this is very fiddly.
OTHER INFO:	Berberine has shown anti-tumour activity. Do not use with liquorice as this counteracts any benefits of Berberis. Darwin's barberry reminds me of living in Tresillian and this grew outside the kitchen window. A lovely house but not the best of times for all who lived there... according to the landlady there were 5 ley-lines running through the house and 2 were classed as 'bad'. The people who lived there before me separated, divorced, got depression and the one before me... died. My first night there, as I closed my bedroom door... I saw an old pink dressing gown hanging there... I screamed!
	If you aren't sure what ley-lines are, they are 'energy lines' between ancient monuments or track ways that link up all around the country. This can be paths that monks would walk, old roads, rivers, hill tops, churches, rock formations, etc.

THE MILLER
Clitopilus prunulus

NAME ORIGIN:	The species *prunulus* means pruinose which means frosted or covered in white powder. *Pilus* means hair in Latin.
FAMILY:	Entolomataceae
EDIBLE PART:	Mushroom
EDIBILITY RATING:	3
WHERE IT'S FOUND:	Deciduous and conifer woodland, likes to grow near ceps
CAUTIONS:	None known but see lookalikes
LOOKALIKES:	Fool's funnel *Clitocybe rivulosa* is the most similar to The miller, and is very poisonous. The miller prefers woodland, fool's funnel prefers grassland. The miller smells like pastry and has pink gills, not white, and gives a pink spore print
MONTH SPAN:	Late summer - autumn

FOOD IDEAS:	Very tasty fried, serve on toast with a squeeze of lemon, with pasta, in soups, stir fry
OTHER INFO:	This is quite a tricky mushroom to begin with as it is not the most easily identifiable

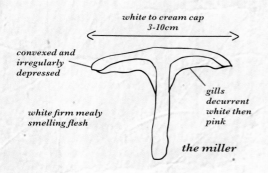

white to cream cap
3-10cm

convexed and
irregularly
depressed

white firm mealy
smelling flesh

gills
decurrent
white then
pink

the miller

SEA HOLLY

Eryngo
Eryngium maritimum

NAME ORIGIN:	*Eryngium* comes from the Greek name for a spiny thistle and *maritimum* means belonging to the coast
FAMILY:	Apiaceae

EDIBLE PART:	Root
EDIBILITY RATING:	3
WHERE IT'S FOUND:	Sand dunes, shingle, coastal
MONTH SPAN:	hz 5 in flower from July – October

FOOD IDEAS:	Roots boiled, roasted or candied
OTHER INFO:	Very rare so do not over harvest and if possible, try and encourage more of it to grow in the wild, perhaps chat to your local environmental societies or National Trust and see if there is anything you can do... maybe collect seed to propagate more to reintroduce in to the wild. This is one of my favourite plants, with such a fabulous rich blue to purple foliage and flowers. I remember the first time I saw Eryngium was when I was about 13 or 14 and went to Abersoch in North Wales with one of my best mates Jo and her family and I saw it for the first time... I was so excited!!!

MARIGOLD

Calendula arvensis **field marigold**
Calendula officinalis **common marigold**

NAME ORIGIN:	*Calendula* comes from the Latin word *calendae* meaning the first day of the month probably alluding to the flowering of the plant throughout the year. *Officinalis* means of the apothecary's shop (medicinal) and *arvensis* means of the fields
FAMILY:	**Asteraceae**
EDIBLE PART:	Flowers, leaves
EDIBILITY RATING:	3
WHERE IT'S FOUND:	Waste ground, gardens, garden escape, fields, roadsides, arable land
CAUTIONS:	Emmenagogue, avoid during pregnancy
MONTH SPAN:	Flowers June - November hz 6.

FOOD IDEAS:	Eat the flowers raw in salads or use as a garnish, eat the leaves raw or cooked (rich in minerals). A tea can be made from the petals and they can be used as a dye.
OTHER INFO:	*Calendula officinalis* made into a hair rinse can be used to give your hair golden highlights. It is very good for soothing skin complaints and healing wounds

SNEEZEWORT
Achillea ptarmica

NAME ORIGIN:	Named after Achilles the Greek hero and *ptarmos* or *ptairo* which comes from the Greek for sneeze as it was dried, powdered and used for snuff
FAMILY:	Asteraceae

EDIBLE PART:	Leaves
EDIBILITY RATING:	2
WHERE IT'S FOUND:	Damp areas, by streams, meadows, marshland, can cope with coastal areas
CAUTIONS:	Emmenagogue, avoid during pregnancy
LOOKALIKES:	It looks like yarrow *Achillea millefolium* but sneezewort has larger, pompom-like flowers that look like little shuttlecocks.
MONTH SPAN:	hz 5, flowers June – October

FOOD IDEAS:	Eat the leaves raw or cooked, used as a flavouring in dishes including salads
OTHER INFO:	Chewing the leaves relieves toothache, the leaves can be used as an insect repellent and the dried powdered leaves can be used as a sneezing powder! It also staunches wounds (styptic).

HOTTENTOT FIG

Carpobrotus edulis

SYNONYM:	*Mesembryanthemum edule*
NAME ORIGIN:	*Carpus* means fruit, *edulis* is edible in Latin and *brotus* is Greek for edible
FAMILY:	Aizoaceae

EDIBLE PART:	Fruit and succulent leaves
EDIBILITY RATING:	3
WHERE IT'S FOUND:	Coastal, especially in the South West
MONTH SPAN:	hz 8, flowers May - July, fruits ripen August - October

FOOD IDEAS:	Leaves raw or cooked, fruits raw, cooked or dried, can be pickled or made into a tart jam
OTHER INFO:	This is a very invasive plant! I love going on the train. My favourite stretch is Teignmouth where you can have treacherous stormy seas spraying one side of the train and on the other side, cliffs covered with hottentot figs - waterfalls of green succulent trails, flecked with vibrant flowers. This is quite a controversial plant as it is invasive but has also been planted to help stabilise cliffs… it is now an offence to introduce this anywhere as it is so invasive!

TANSY

Tanacetum vulgare

SYNONYM:	*Tanacetum audiberti, Chrysanthemum vulgare, Chrysanthemum tanacetum*
NAME ORIGIN:	**Tanacetum possibly derives from the Greek 'athanatos' which means immortal, referring to the long lasting flowers and *vulgare* means common**
FAMILY:	**Asteraceae**

EDIBLE PART:	Leaves, flowers
EDIBILITY RATING:	2
WHERE IT'S FOUND:	Hedgerows, waste ground, can tolerate maritime conditions
CAUTIONS:	Abortifacient - avoid if pregnant. Avoid eating in large quantities as possibly poisonous. There is conflicting information on this plant as in some sources it says do not take internally whereas others suggest eating the flowers and using the leaves as a nutmeg substitute. I think the key is eat in moderation and you only need a few leaves as it has a strong flavour.
LOOKALIKES:	Related to feverfew but tansy leaves are more feathery and toothed
MONTH SPAN:	Flowers July - October, hz 4

FOOD IDEAS:	Eat the leaves raw or cooked, eat flowers in salads, etc. Use it to flavour cakes, omelettes, puddings, goes well with almonds, rosewater, ginger – you only need 4 small leaves to flavour any dessert.

ROASTED SOLE WITH SAGE BUTTER

2 Dover soles
3/4 cup of butter
1/4 cup plain flour
1 large handful sage leaves
juice of a lemon
1/3 glass of white wine
Seasoning

Preheat the oven to 220 degrees C. In a large frying pan suitable for putting in the oven, melt half the butter. Dust the sole in flour and fry on both sides until crisp and brown. Pop the pan in the oven for about 7 minutes until cooked through. Remove the fish (keeping it warm) and using the same pan return it to the hob, and melt the rest of the butter. Fry the sage leaves until crisp and remove with a slotted spoon and put to one side. Add the wine and lemon juice when the butter is turning brown, stirring well and allowing to just simmer, seasoning to taste. Serve the sole with the sage leaves on top and pour the butter sauce over the fish.

DOVER SOLE

Solea solea

NAME ORIGIN:	**The name *solea* possibly derives from the Latin word for sun**
FAMILY:	**Soleidae**
EDIBLE PART:	Flesh
EDIBILITY RATING:	4
WHERE IT'S FOUND:	Sandy bottom sea, off piers
CAUTIONS:	Avoid if you have fish allergies
LOOKALIKES:	It looks like flatfish, like flounder and plaice but is larger
MONTH SPAN:	All year round, best July – February
FOOD IDEAS:	Strip off the upper skin and bake whole, grill, roast, pan fry, strip and cover in flour, egg and breadcrumbs then deep fry for goujons. Delicious with flavoured butters
OTHER INFO:	Dover sole likes lugworm as bait. They have small mouths so use a size 2-6 hook. As they swim in shoals, use multi-hook rigs and keep the bait as close to the sea bed as possible

CHICORY

Cichorum intybus

NAME ORIGIN:	**Kichore comes from the Greek for root vegetable. Another name is succory who was the beautiful young girl who spurned the amorous intentions of the sun and so was turned into a plant that must stare aloft towards the sun during daylight hours**
FAMILY:	**Asteraceae**
EDIBLE PART:	Flowers, leaves, roots
EDIBILITY RATING:	4
WHERE IT'S FOUND:	Arable land, meadows
CAUTIONS:	Excess use could affect eyesight by impairing retina function
MONTH SPAN:	Flowers July - October hz 3

FOOD IDEAS:	Forcing the plant by shutting out light (put a bucket or something over the plant) and this reduces the bitterness in the leaves. In winter the leaves are less bitter anyway. Eat leaves raw or cooked, eat the flowers raw. Young boiled roots (up to 2 years old) eaten as a vegetable or roasted to make a coffee substitute.
OTHER INFO:	Chicory is collected in strict silence on 25th July which is the day of St James. If you lay the flowers on an anthill, they supposedly turn a brilliant red! This is probably due to the formic acid that ants secrete

RASPBERRIES WITH WHITE CHOCOLATE AND AMARETTO

Adapted from a Nigella
Lawson recipe

Enough raspberries to serve
each person 12+ each
1 large bar white chocolate
1 large shot amaretto

Freeze your raspberries. In a bain marie (place a heatproof bowl above a saucepan of water) get the water simmering, break up the white chocolate into the bowl adding the amaretto and melt, stirring to mix together. Put the frozen raspberries in bowls and pour over the chocolate sauce immediately. The heat from the sauce melts the raspberries and turns the sauce fudgy with the coldness.

RASPBERRY

Rubus idaeus

NAME ORIGIN:	*Rubus* is the old Roman name, probably from *ruber* meaning red and *idaeus* meaning from Mount Ida
FAMILY:	**Rosaceae**
EDIBLE PART:	Fruit, leaves
EDIBILITY RATING:	5
WHERE IT'S FOUND:	Moist ground, woodland, hedgerows
MONTH SPAN:	hz 3, in leaf April - November, flowers June - August, fruits July - September

FOOD IDEAS:	Use the dried leaves to make tea, the fruits raw or cooked, made into jam, puddings, etc. The roots can be cooked and eaten but need a lot of boiling, the young shoots peeled and eaten raw or cooked (in spring). Raspberry liqueur, cordial, meringue roulade with raspberry filling, sorbet, mousse, chocolate and raspberry torte, raspberry vinaigrette.
OTHER INFO:	Raspberry leaf contains fragarine which acts on the pelvic muscles. Raspberry leaf tea is recommended for pregnant women in the last 3 months of pregnancy and during childbirth. It is also good at treating painful period cramps.

'SHE WORE A RASPBERRY BERET... THE KIND YOU'D FIND IN A SECOND-HAND STORE, RASPBERRY BERET... AND IF IT WAS WARM SHE WOULDN'T WEAR MUCH MORE... RASPBERRY BERET, I THINK I LOVE HER'

Prince

BROWN SHRIMP

Crangon crangon

NAME ORIGIN:	Comes from Middle English 'shrimpe', meaning to shrivel up or wrinkle.
FAMILY:	**Crangonidae**
EDIBLE PART:	Meat
EDIBILITY RATING:	5
WHERE IT'S FOUND:	Sandy and muddy estuaries
CAUTIONS:	Gather from a clean area, avoid after heavy rainfall. Avoid if allergic to shellfish.
LOOKALIKES:	Prawns!
MONTH SPAN:	March - June, September - November, although pretty much like mussels ('r' in the month) so keep trying through the winter!

FOOD IDEAS:	Paella, seafood chowder, lemon and shrimp spaghetti, potted shrimp. Ideally only keep shrimps that once cooked, YOU will be able to actually peel - the tiniest ones are best thrown back to live another day but if you have got really small shrimp, add them to a seafood bisque to release the flavours but that you will strain and remove the shells from the dish.
OTHER INFO:	The difference between shrimps and prawns is not size as many people think (size isn't everything), as prawns have babies too. The main differences are that shrimps have lamellar gills (layered or linear looking) where prawns have branching, shrimps have 2 pairs of claws while prawns have 3 pairs. Both prawns and shrimps have 3 segments of abdomen but a shrimp's middle section will protrude over first and third segment, where a prawn's middle section only protrudes over the third section. For shrimping, head to tidal rivers with plenty of seaweed for cover, especially bladderwrack. The best time to catch them is when the tide is coming in from low tide, about a couple of hours in, where the sea is coming over the sand and seaweeds. If you don't want to buy a

shrimping net, you can easily make one by creating a D shaped net with the flat bit at the base and use netting with small holes. Use it by pushing the net through seaweedy shallow water, maybe don a pair of wellies and walk with it, then scoop up and keep your fingers crossed! Once you have found the best shrimping places, tell as few people as possible. The term prawn and shrimp is used interchangeably - you eat them in the same way, so hey? Why split hairs?? By the way, when shrimping, beware of catching weaver fish, also known as sticklers, as they give a painful sting. If stung, put the effected area in as hot water as you can handle - in the case of anaphylactic shock or serious swelling, call 999.

prawn ——

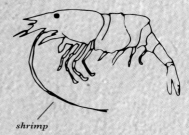

shrimp

POTTED SHRIMP

For a pint of shelled shrimps, use
4 oz butter
2 bay leaves
a generous pinch of cayenne pepper
juice of half a lemon
season to taste

Potted shrimp - so delicious! How to deal with the shrimps when you have got them home... I keep mine in a bucket of shallow water so when I get in my kitchen, I put the plug in the sink, put the colander in and pour the bucket in to the colander. Pick out any bits of debris such as leaves, seaweed, stones. Give them a quick rinse and get some water boiling in a large saucepan. If any shrimps have escaped into the sink, scoop them up with a slotted spoon and put them in the colander. When you are ready, swiftly pour the shrimps into the boiling water and cook until pink which will take a maximum of 5 minutes. Drain, put to one side and leave to cool before setting about peeling them. Pinch the head off, then peel the shell off from the belly up, then gently pinch the tail and tug the last bit off.....

Melt 3 oz of the butter in a frying pan, and add the rest of the ingredients, stirring through for a couple of minutes. Remove the bay leaves and pour the shrimp mixture into a clean sterilized jar. Melt the remaining 1 oz of butter, skimming off the foamy bit to leave clarified butter. Pour this over the top and serve immediately with bread and butter or refrigerate.

COMMON PRAWN
Palaemon serratus

NAME ORIGIN:	The species name *serratus* means serrated and *Palaemon* is possibly named after the Greek *Palaemon*, who was an argonaut (with Jason in the quest to find the golden fleece in Colchis (where saffron and crocus originate)), the son of Heracles and grandson of Zeus. The other origin of the name is also from Greek mythology – Melicertes was the son of Prince Athamas and Ino. Hera drove Prince Athamas mad and he pursued Ino and Melicertes so she threw herself and her son into the sea. Both of them were turned into marine deities; Melicertes became Palaemon and is often depicted as a boy riding on a dolphin's back.
FAMILY:	Palaemonidae
EDIBLE PART:	Meat
EDIBILITY RATING:	5
WHERE IT'S FOUND:	Rocky crevices
CAUTIONS:	Gather from clean areas and avoid if you are allergic to shellfish. Ask the advice of your doctor if you are pregnant.
LOOKALIKES:	Shrimps! The difference between shrimps and prawns is not size as many people think (size isn't everything), as prawns have babies too. The main differences are that shrimps have lamellar gills (layered or linear looking) where prawns are branching, shrimps have 2 pairs of claws while prawns have 3 pairs and both prawns and shrimps have 3 segments of abdomen but a shrimp's middle section will protrude over first and third segment, where a prawn's middle section only protrudes over the third section. The term prawn and shrimp is used interchangeably - you eat them in the same way, so hey? Why split hairs?? By the way, when catching prawns, beware of catching weaver fish, also known as sticklers, as they give a painful sting. If stung, put the affected area in as hot water as you can handle - in the case of anaphylactic shock or serious swelling, call 999

Fry, grill, barbeque, poach. Either raw or cooked, when it comes to peeling, hold the body with one hand and twist the head off with the other. When they are cooked you can pinch the tail end of the body and occasionally pull the shell off gently like a sock. When raw, work your way from the head end down the body by unwrapping the layers from the belly and off the back of the body.

OTHER INFO:

For shrimping, head to tidal rivers with plenty of seaweed for cover, especially bladder wrack. The best time to catch them is when the tide is coming in from low tide, about a couple of hours in, where the sea is coming over the sand and seaweeds. If you don't want to buy a shrimping net, you can easily make one by creating a D shaped net with the flat bit at the base and use netting with small holes. Use it by pushing the net through seaweedy shallow water, maybe don a pair of wellies and walk with it, then scoop up and keep your fingers crossed! Once you have found the best shrimping places, tell as few people as possible. Prawns like rock pools and are really quite seasonal, preferring autumn.

GUMBO!
(Serves 4)

1 tbsp olive oil
a knob of butter
1 red pepper deseeded and chopped
2 celery sticks, sliced
2 oz rindless bacon
2 onions
3 cloves of garlic
1 tbsp plain flour
1 ltr vegetable stock
1 tbsp smoked paprika
1 tin of chopped tomatoes
a tied bunch of thyme
3 bay leaves
a handful of fresh parsley, chopped
2 tsp Worcestershire sauce
1 tbsp cornflour
1 lb prawns
2 oz green beans
Seasoning
a baguette warmed in the oven to make it delicious and crusty

In a large frying pan, heat the oil and butter. Peel and dice the onions and add along with the celery and pepper until soft and colouring up. Slice up the bacon, peel and finely chop the garlic and add both to the pan for a couple of minutes then add the flour and paprika until coated and cook for a minute.

Using a balloon whisk, add the stock, stirring well to prevent lumps. Once combined, add the tinned tomatoes, thyme, bay, parsley and Worcestershire sauce. In a cup put the cornflour and decant about a tablespoon or so of liquid from the pan. Mix until well combined, then add to the pan. Leave to simmer until thickened.

Peel the prawns (de-vein if necessary), chop the green beans and add both, simmering in the mixture until the prawns are pink and the beans are cooked. Take off the heat, remove the thyme and bay and serve with a crusty baguette.

RED CLOVER
Trifolium pratense

NAME ORIGIN:	*Trifolium* means three-leaved and *pratense* means meadow
FAMILY:	**Fabaceae**
EDIBLE PART:	Flowers and leaves
EDIBILITY RATING:	3
WHERE IT'S FOUND:	Grassland, meadows, pastures
CAUTIONS:	Clover can sometimes be diseased and contain toxic alkaloids but show no symptoms! Seeds are said to contain trypsin inhibitors which can prevent certain enzymes digesting proteins, but foods from the same family like soya beans and lima beans also contain this - as with everything, eat in moderation.
LOOKALIKES:	Oxalis can look similar but are edible and have an apple-skin tang
MONTH SPAN:	Flowers May - September, hz 6

FOOD IDEAS:	The young leaves before the plant flowers can be used in salads, cooked like spinach, added to dishes, soups, and the dried leaves can be used in baking to impart a vanilla like flavour. The flowers and seed pods can be dried and ground into a powder and used like flour, young flowers can be eaten raw or dried and used to make a tea. The cooked root can be eaten as a vegetable.
OTHER INFO:	Kids used to like eating butter, sugar and clover flower sandwiches - maybe time for a revival!

BLACKCURRANT
Ribes nigrum

SYNONYM:	*Ribes pauciflorum*
NAME ORIGIN:	*Nigrum* means black referring to the fruit, possibly from the Arabic *ribas* which was an acidic plant used by physicians
FAMILY:	Grossulariaceae

EDIBLE PART:	Fruit, leaves
EDIBILITY RATING:	5

MONTH SPAN:	In leaf from March - November, flowers April - May, fruits July - August
FOOD IDEAS:	Use the dried leaves for tea, eat the fruit raw or cooked. It is great for jam, ice cream, sorbet, tarts, sauces, liqueurs (crème de cassis), crumbles, creamy or fresh desserts. Use the fresh leaves as a flavouring – they also make an excellent sorbet. Blackcurrants are a key ingredient for summer pudding.
OTHER INFO:	Blackcurrants are high in vitamin C and also pectins which means jams and jellies set easily without additional pectin. If you are making a jam or jelly, let the liquid drip through muslin without squeezing the bag, otherwise your jam will be cloudy. During WWII, vitamin C was quite hard to come by as oranges and other vitamin C rich fruits weren't available. Blackcurrant crop production grew dramatically and in 1942 a government scheme offered children under the age of 2 blackcurrant syrup free of charge.

BLACKCURRANT
ICE LOLLIES

4 cups blackcurrants (washed)
juice of a lemon
4 tbsp honey
1/2 cup of fruit juice (apple or
orange juice is good)

Blend all the ingredients in a food processor and pour into ice lolly moulds. If you want super smooth ice lollies, then pass through a sieve. Freeze.

OTHER INFO:	They must be 65mm minimum across the carapace, otherwise put them back. In parts of Europe velvet swimming crabs are being over-fished so only gather them sustainably and only enough for yourself.

VELVET SWIMMING CRAB
Necora puber

NAME ORIGIN:	*Puber* means downy and *nécora* is Spanish for small edible crab.
FAMILY:	**Portunidae**
EDIBLE PART:	Meat
EDIBILITY RATING:	4
WHERE IT'S FOUND:	Rocky shores
CAUTIONS:	Avoid if pregnant and avoiding shellfish, avoid if you have shellfish allergies
LOOKALIKES:	Velvet swimming crabs are quite easy to identify with their downy shells, back legs are paddles and devil-red eyes. Sandy swimming crabs (*Liocarcinus depurator*) are similar but have white spots on their shell and sometimes legs.
MONTH SPAN:	All year round

FOOD IDEAS:	These crabs have a fair amount of meat for such a small crab and you can eat all of the flesh, just avoid the dead man's fingers which are the feathery gills. They are not harmful in the least, just indigestible and you wouldn't want to get one stuck in your throat! Boil, barbeque, use the shell and all other parts for making soup or bisque because you'll sieve it.
RECIPE:	Delicious as they are or why not try crab linguini with lemon, garlic and chilli or with fennel and white wine? Boil the linguini and at the same time, gently fry the garlic and chilli, add lemon zest, add the linguini to toss in the flavours. Add the crab meat and a glug of wine, let it simmer, add fennel and season. Add cream or crème fraîche for a creamy linguini.

CALIFORNIAN POPPY
Eschscholzia californica

SYNONYM:	*Eschscholzia douglasii*
NAME ORIGIN:	*Californica* means Californian and the genus is named after Dr. J F von Eschscholtz who was a naturalist and physician
FAMILY:	Papaveraceae

EDIBLE PART:	Petals, seeds and cooked leaves
EDIBILITY RATING:	2
WHERE IT'S FOUND:	Garden escape, sunny position
CAUTIONS:	It comes from a toxic family, but none specifically for *Eschscholzia*
LOOKALIKES:	Californian poppies are pretty distinctive, with 4 orange petals, long blue/green seed pods and glaucous foliage. You can get some stunning cultivated varieties with varying coloured petals.

MONTH SPAN:	Flowers July - September, seeds ripen August – September
FOOD IDEAS:	Use the petals in salads, savoury dishes or desserts, eat the leaves cooked, add the seeds to dishes
OTHER INFO:	If you feed hyperactive children *Eschscholzia* petals, it is meant to chill them out… anyone want to test out the theory? It has also been used to help prevent bed wetting and insomnia.

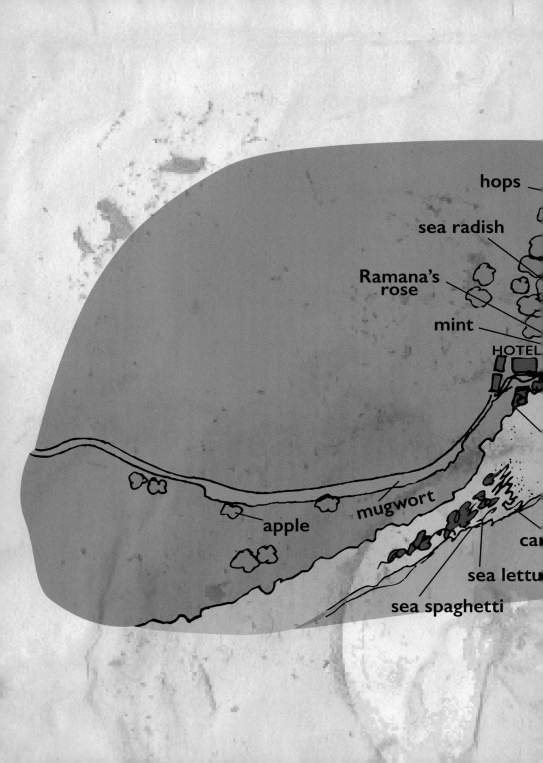

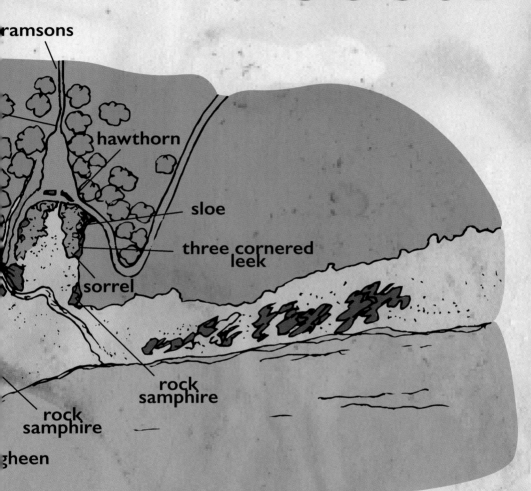

ramsons

hawthorn

sloe

three cornered
leek

sorrel

rock
samphire

rock
samphire

gheen

COMMON GARDEN SNAIL (ESCARGOT!)

Cornu aspersum

SYNONYM	*Helix aspersa*
NAME ORIGIN:	*Helix* refers to the form of the spiralling shell (Fibonacci) and *aspersa* means strewn or scattered. *Cornu* is 'horn' in Latin.
FAMILY:	Helicidae
EDIBLE PART:	Meat
EDIBILITY RATING:	3
WHERE IT'S FOUND:	Garden, especially on a damp night!
LOOKALIKES:	Slugs!
MONTH SPAN:	You can always find these as they are always out to annoy gardeners. In the winter when it gets really cold, they will create a membrane that seals up the hole in their shell to prevent frost damage. They also do this when the weather is really dry.
FOOD IDEAS:	Snails are pretty good to eat when they are prepared well. All you need to do is collect up as many as you want to try - if this is your first time, just try a handful, although any gardener will be happy to see the back of them. A fish tank is ideal, but anything that you can keep them in that they can't escape from but can also breathe is suitable. To purge them will remove their sliminess which is the main off-putting part about them. To do this you need to feed them a diet of lettuce, cabbage, apple or vine leaves - the reason they are slimy is down to what they eat. Slugs can have the same treatment, but I just can't bring myself to try them! Also try stir frying or boiling. They go well with creamy aniseed flavours, such as pernod cream.

RECIPE:	Purge the snails on foods such as vine leaves, apples, sunflower seeds, lettuce, etc. for a week. Remove their membrane that seals up the hole, wash them well then put them in salted water with vinegar and a spoonful of flour, purge them for 48 hours (don't give them any food or water), wash them again thoroughly then they are ready for cooking – simmering for 5 minutes. Now you can use them in whatever recipe you wish to try. If you want to try garlic butter snails, put the prepared snails back in clean shells, push butter mixed with garlic and parsley into the shell and bake/grill for a few minutes, shell-hole-side up.
OTHER INFO:	Paris, Chartier! This restaurant in the heart of Paris is the best place to try snails for the first time (actual my first time was in the gorgeous fishing village of Mevagissey in Cornwall). The only tip though, do you like garlic? And if given the option of 6 or 12, go for 6 as they can become an overwhelming entity that can pleasure but defeat you all in one mouthful. You need to check the snail is mature before collecting them and to do so, all you need to do is to check their shell opening to see if it has a hard lip or soft lip – if it is hard, then it is mature enough, otherwise leave it to keep growing. The slimy secretions of *Cornu aspersum* have become really popular recently as a key ingredient in skin care products, due to its regenerative effects. When stressed, they produce antioxidant enzymes Superoxide dismutase and Glutathione S-transferase which help with scarring, wound tissue, discolouration and wrinkles.

ANNUAL SEABLIGHT
Suaeda maritima

NAME ORIGIN:	*Suaeda* means composition in Latin and the species *maritima* means maritime/coastal.
FAMILY:	Chenopodiaceae
EDIBLE PART:	Young leaves or shoots
EDIBILITY RATING:	3
WHERE IT'S FOUND:	Salt marshes, coastal
MONTH SPAN:	Flowers July - October, seeds ripen August - October

FOOD IDEAS:	Raw or cooked young leaves or shoots, steamed, used as a sea vegetable.
OTHER INFO:	Growing to about a foot tall, this knotted red stemmed plant is quite delicious eaten as it is or steamed, and grows throughout the UK. It's often overlooked as you tend to be looking for the more obvious marsh samphire or sea purslane but try and get your eye in to spot this one as it is just as tasty.

PICKEREL WEED
Pontederia cordata

NAME ORIGIN:	A *pickerel is* a North American pike (fish). The genus was named by Linnaeus after Italian botanist Giulio Pontedera and *cordata* means heart-shaped referring to the leaves.
FAMILY:	**Pontederiaceae**

EDIBLE PART:	Seeds, young leaf stalks
EDIBILITY RATING:	3
WHERE IT'S FOUND:	Wetland areas, lakes, ponds
CAUTIONS:	Collect from a clean source
LOOKALIKES:	Nothing else that I know of has a purple flower spike and long heart-shaped leaves.
MONTH SPAN:	Flowers July - September

FOOD IDEAS:	The seeds are ready to collect when they easily come off the flower spike. Try them raw, boiled, roasted or dehydrate them to make flour. The lightly roasted seeds are very tasty. Eat the young leaf stalks raw or boiled, use like spinach, put in salads, etc.
OTHER INFO:	This beautiful marginal aquatic is native to America.

WILD MARJORAM

Oregano
Origanum vulgare

NAME ORIGIN:	*Oros* is Greek for mountain, *ganos* means joy (the plant was made by Aphrodite to symbolize happiness) and *vulgare* means common
FAMILY:	Lamiaceae

EDIBLE PART:	Flowers and leaves
EDIBILITY RATING:	5
WHERE IT'S FOUND:	Grassland, scrub
CAUTIONS:	Emmenagogue so avoid during early stages of pregnancy (in the mint family).
MONTH SPAN:	Flowers form July - September, seeds ripen August - October

FOOD IDEAS:	Amazing with tomato sauces, salad dressings and cheese
OTHER INFO:	The dried herb can taste even better than the fresh, and it stores well - I believe the Italians prefer it mostly dried in their dishes. Wild marjoram and oregano are the same plant (same species), but the climate can make a huge difference in strength of flavour. A natural antiseptic, oregano oil helps treat skin complaints.

TOMATO AND OREGANO SAUCE

Perfect for bolognaise or pizza bases

1-2tbsp olive oil
1 onion
1 clove of garlic
1 tin of chopped tomatoes
1/2 vegetable stock cube
1 good handful oregano
seasoning
(glug of red wine optional)

Peel and finely chop the onion and garlic. Heat the olive oil in a frying pan and fry the onion until soft. Add the garlic, stirring for 30 seconds and add the red wine if using it now, simmer and add the tin of tomatoes and the stock cube (just the tomatoes, not the tin itself!). Roughly chop the oregano and add, stirring and leaving to simmer and thicken. Season to taste. For a pizza sauce, simmer and stir until it is really thick. For bolognaise, I use celery in it which I add with the onions to soften.

CORN POPPY
Field poppy
Papaver rhoeas

NAME ORIGIN:	*Papaver* is the Latin name for poppy and the Celtic word papa means gruel/porridge because the seeds were added to children's porridge to help them sleep! Pappa is also the Latin word for food or milk. The species *rhoeas* comes from *rhoia* which is the Greek for pomegranate (and *rhoeas* means red?) because the fruits resemble them. The word poppy comes from the French poupée meaning doll, because dolls were made from them.
FAMILY:	**Papaveraceae**

EDIBLE PART:	Seeds, petals, leaves
EDIBILITY RATING:	4
WHERE IT'S FOUND:	Cultivated land, waste ground, disturbed soil, fields
CAUTIONS:	It has very low toxicity (trace opiates) so you would have to consume massive quantities to have any effect. It is an emmenagogue so avoid consuming any parts during pregnancy.
MONTH SPAN:	Flowers June - August, seeds ripen August – September

FOOD IDEAS:	Use the seeds in baking bread, cakes, etc. Eat the leaves raw or cooked, only before the seed heads have formed. Eat the petals in salads or as a garnish for sweet or savoury dishes. Try making a syrup from the petals for drinks or puddings.
OTHER INFO:	The field poppy is the memorial flower of veterans in World War I. After the devastation of battle fields from the conflicts, field poppies grow naturally in disturbed soil and therefore grew around the bodies of the fallen soldiers, the scarlet of the petals symbolising the bloodshed. The Royal British Legion adopted the poppy as their symbol and collects money for those serving the British Armed Forces.

PARMESAN AND POPPY SEED STRAWS

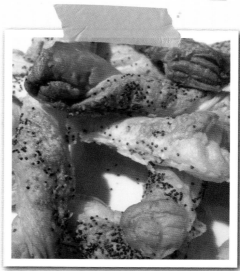

I pack of puff pastry
I egg
2 tbsp poppy seeds
2 tbsp finely grated parmesan

Preheat the oven to 180 degrees C. Beat the egg. Roll the pastry to 3 mm thick and cut into strips 1 cm wide - length optional. Lay the pastry strips on a baking tray (on greased parchment) and brush on the beaten egg. Sprinkle on the parmesan and poppy seeds. Gently twist the strips a few times and bake for 15 - 20 minutes until golden.

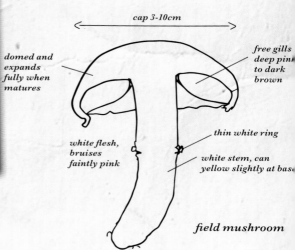

cap 3-10cm

domed and
expands
fully when
matures

free gills
deep pink
to dark
brown

white flesh,
bruises
faintly pink

thin white ring

white stem, can
yellow slightly at base

field mushroom

STUFFED MUSHROOMS WITH CHUNKY SALSA

(Serves 4 as a starter)

4 large field mushrooms
1/2 cup butter
2 tbsp olive oil
3 cloves garlic, peeled and finely chopped
1 large handful of flat leaf parsley, finely chopped
1 tbsp finely chopped mozzarella
1 tbsp finely chopped cheddar
2 slices of bread turned into breadcrumbs
1 avocado
12-14 cherry tomatoes
juice of 1/2 a lemon
seasoning

Preheat the oven to 200 degrees C. Wipe clean the mushrooms to remove any dirt, don't wash them as they act like sponges. Mix the butter, garlic and parsley together in a bowl with a little seasoning. Place the mushrooms on a baking tray, gills facing up and fill each mushroom with the butter filling. In a separate bowl, loosely mix the cheese and breadcrumbs and top each mushroom. Drizzle with olive oil and pop in the oven to bake for about 10-15 minutes, or until the breadcrumbs are toasted and the cheese melted. Meanwhile, dice the avocado and cherry tomatoes, mixing together in a bowl with the lemon juice and season. Serve the mushroom with the salsa.

FIELD MUSHROOM

Agaricus campestris

NAME ORIGIN:	The species *campestris* means field and *Agaricus* comes from *Agari* which is a district of Sarmatia.
FAMILY:	**Agaricaceae**

EDIBLE PART:	Mushroom
EDIBILITY RATING:	4
WHERE IT'S FOUND:	Grassland (often grows in rings)
LOOKALIKES:	Yellow stainer, or immature death caps, white *Clitocybe* or destroying angels! The yellow stainer is *Agaricus xanthodermus* so is related but the main thing is when you cut it, especially at the base it colours up a strong yellow quite quickly. It also doesn't smell great, especially when cooked. Immature death caps (*Amanita phalloides*) and destroying angels (*Amanita virosa*) are both amanitas and have white gills and a bulbous base from which the stem grows – *Agaricus* have pink to brown gills and don't grow out of a sac. *Clitocybe* have decurrent gills and as they mature, become funnel-shaped.

MONTH SPAN:	Summer - autumn
FOOD IDEAS:	Eat it raw or cooked, make it in to soup, pan fried, stuffed, stir fry, mushroom and potato croquettes, bruschetta con funghi (they go great with garlic, parsley, tarragon).

SEA ROCKET
Cakile maritima

SYNONYM	*Cakile edentula, Bunias cakile*
NAME ORIGIN:	The species name *maritima* means maritime and *Cakile* derives from the old Arabic kakeleh, qaqila or qaqulla meaning cardamom.
FAMILY:	**Brassicaceae**

EDIBLE PART:	Flowers, young leaves, immature seed pods
EDIBILITY RATING:	2
WHERE IT'S FOUND:	Coastal, sand and shingle
CAUTIONS:	It contains erucic acid which should be avoided by young children
MONTH SPAN:	(hz 6) flowers June - August, seeds ripen August – September

FOOD IDEAS:	Eat the young leaves raw or cooked, eat the stems, flower buds and immature seed pods
OTHER INFO:	Sea rocket is rich in vitamin C. The plant can be quite strong and bitter, with a potent mustard flavour. This is one I identified from my Wild Food book (Roger Phillips) when I was about 14. I had headed to the beach by myself with my rucksack, imitation Swiss army pen knife, peanut butter and jam sandwiches and my Wild Food book. It was the best day ever! I whittled a fork and spoon, discovered how sea salt formed salt crystals and spotted this plant. I was in heaven!

GREY MULLET
Mugil sp.

FAMILY:	**Mugilidae**
EDIBLE PART:	Meat
EDIBILITY RATING:	5
WHERE IT'S FOUND:	Tidal estuaries, harbours
CAUTIONS:	None known – avoid if you're allergic to fish!
MONTH SPAN:	Spring, summer, autumn

FOOD IDEAS:	Baked whole on an open fire is pretty hard to beat! Bake stuffed in the oven or fillet and grill. Pan fry, add to seafood soups or chowders, paellas, etc
RECIPE:	This doesn't really need a recipe - the best way to eat it is al fresco along with a little wild camping! Get a fire going and put rocks around it to hold a grill over the fire. Gut the mullet and pop on the grill, turning to cook both sides. Eat! No seasoning, no sauces, maybe just a bap or crusty baguette for a mullet burger... so moist, so sweet, so good!
OTHER INFO:	Jordy John is the best at catching mullet. I think it is possibly my favourite fish! We have an island that we camp on that we call John's Island which is the most beautiful place and also where John and Caroline got married. For my birthday a few years ago, we had a pirate camping session where I did treasure maps and hid treasure - try it some time - it is the best!!! Anyway, John caught mullet with his casting net and cooked it on our open fire...wow!

SAND SEDGE

Carex arenaria

SYNONYM:	*Carex spadicea*
NAME ORIGIN:	**The genus is the Latin name for some sedges and the Latin word *arena* means sand**
FAMILY:	**Cyperaceae**
EDIBLE PART:	Roots and seed
EDIBILITY RATING:	2
WHERE IT'S FOUND:	Dunes
LOOKALIKES:	Other dune grasses can look similar but the sand sedge has slightly stiff, star-like, almost rosette shaped shoots which are dark green and grow from a creeping stolon and appear in straight lines. As the outer leaves age, they can become curled or wavy.
MONTH SPAN:	(hz 7) flowers May - July, seeds ripen July – August
FOOD IDEAS:	Cooked roots, seeds as a carb supplement
OTHER INFO:	Sand sedge is one of the first plants to start colonising sand dunes and is very important in stabilisation.

BEACH PEA

Beach vetchling

Lathyrus japonicus ssp. *maritimus*

SYNONYMS:	*Lathyrus maritimus*
NAME ORIGIN:	*Lathyrus* is the Greek name for these leguminous plants, *japonicus* means from Japan and *maritimus* means it is coastal
FAMILY:	Fabaceae
EDIBLE PART:	Immature and mature seeds
EDIBILITY RATING:	2
WHERE IT'S FOUND:	Coastal, shingle beaches
CAUTIONS:	The seed contains a toxic amino-acid which, in large quantities, can cause a very serious disease of the nervous system known as 'lathyrism'. The seed is said to be perfectly safe and very nutritious in small quantities, but don't consume too often!!
MONTH SPAN:	(hz 3) flowers May - August, seeds ripen August - October

FOOD IDEAS:	Eat the raw immature seeds or cook them like peas. The mature seeds can be sprouted or cooked but will mostly taste a little bitter.
OTHER INFO:	This plant is rare so please be conservative with what you pick.

WILD CARROT
Daucus carota

NAME ORIGIN:	*Daucus* is the ancient Greek name for carrot and *carota* means red roots. I always picture ladies that are called Dorcas to have carrot-red hair. Wild carrot is sometimes called Queen Anne's lace but *Ammi* sp. can also have this common name.
FAMILY:	**Apiaceae**
EDIBLE PART:	Root, flower head, seed
EDIBILITY RATING:	3
WHERE IT'S FOUND:	Coastal, grassland, cultivated ground
CAUTIONS:	Wild carrot is an emmenagogue, and carrot sap and foliage can cause photosensitivity (and dermatitis) in some people. The root is also said to induce uterine contractions so avoid during pregnancy. The seeds have been used as a 'morning after' contraceptive as they are abortifacient.
LOOKALIKES:	There are quite a few in the Apiaceae or carrot family, but this has feathery leaves and a concave flower head, often with a solitary pink flower in the centre of the flower cluster. Hemlock *Conium maculatum* is similar but has purple blotches on the stems and hairless, whereas wild carrot is covered in hairs, has no purple blotches and the tiny flowers are packed together tightly.
MONTH SPAN:	Flowers June – August

FOOD IDEAS:	Try deep fried flower heads as decorative delicious additions to a meal, try the root cooked, eaten raw like cultivated carrots or dried, roasted and used as a coffee substitute. The leaves can be used as a garnish or flavouring. The seeds can be used as a spice and the fruits can be collected and dried then used as a carrot/coriander flavour. I think the flavour is quite reminiscent of Christmas pudding.

Carrot leaf has become quite 'fashionable' to use as a decorative condiment or flavouring in dishes. Carrots are very good for us – they contain Beta carotene (vitamin A), vitamin K, vitamin C, biotin and other minerals and carbohydrates. Eating carrots helps you see in the dark! This is actually true as the nutrients within a carrot help promote healthy eyes. Carrots were originally white, yellow and purple but never orange. It wasn't until an orange variety with high amounts of Beta-carotene was bred in honour of a man named William of Orange who led the Dutch in revolt.

WILD CARROT SYRUP

2 cups sugar
1 cup water
3 cups wild carrot (use any part
– leaves, flowers, stem, etc.)

Roughly chop the wild carrot and put it in a large bowl. Combine the water and sugar in a saucepan and heat until it simmers and the sugar has dissolved. Pour it over the wild carrot, cover and leave to infuse for 24 hours. Strain using muslin and bottle. Try it in cocktails or mocktails but see cautions.

CROCOSMIA

Montbretia
Crocosmia aurea

SYNONYM:	*Tritonia aurea*
NAME ORIGIN:	*Aurea* means gold and *crocos* or *krokos* means saffron or crocus as the flowers can be used like saffron and *osme* means odour.
FAMILY:	**Iridaceae**

EDIBLE PART:	Flowers
EDIBILITY RATING:	2
WHERE IT'S FOUND	Gardens, garden escapee
MONTH SPAN:	July - August (hz 7)

FOOD IDEAS:	Use the petals as a saffron substitute, add them to rice dishes for splashes of colour, add them to cakes, biscuits, salads, etc.
OTHER INFO:	I grew up in Singapore and strangely so does this plant – not just in temperate regions. Also known as montbretia, my friend Catherine and I would start off with a rolling competition across the lawn and back, then jump in the pool, itching like mad, then use crocosmia flowers as a body dye, as well as hibiscus and other tropical adornments… we were so jazzy…

MEADOW CLARY
Salvia pratensis

NAME ORIGIN:	*Salveo* means I heal in Latin and *pratensis* means meadow. The genus is the Latin name used by Pliny
FAMILY:	**Lamiaceae**

EDIBLE PART:	Leaves
EDIBILITY RATING:	1
WHERE IT'S FOUND:	Grassland (chalk), rare to find
MONTH SPAN:	Flowers July - August (hz 3)

FOOD IDEAS:	Meadow clary can be used as a sage substitute, a condiment and as a flavouring for wines or beers
OTHER INFO:	The word clary comes from 'clear eye' because it was used for clearing or soothing eyes. As with clary sage *Salvia sclarea*, don't be tempted to have a go applying it to your eyes as both plants have small hairs that could irritate, so leave it to the experts. This plant has declined over the years so is classed as 'Near Threatened' so as with all 'wild' plants, never uproot or damage them. We are seeing meadow clary a little more often because of popular wild flower seed mixes so why don't you start rewilding areas you own with this beautiful blue-flowering plant?

CHOP-SUEY GREENS; CORN MARIGOLD

Chrysanthemum coronarium; Chrysanthemum segetum

SYNONYM:	*Glebionis coronaria* and *Glebionis segetum* are the most recent, so technically *C. coronarium* and *C. segetum* are the synonyms
NAME ORIGIN:	*Chrysos* is Greek for gold, *anthemon* for flower, *coronarium* means crown-like referring to the 'crown' of outer petals (coronation, corona) and *segetum* means of corn fields
FAMILY:	**Asteraceae**
EDIBLE PART:	Flowers, fresh young shoots, cooked leaves
EDIBILITY RATING:	3
WHERE IT'S FOUND:	Cultivated land
CAUTIONS:	For *Chrysanthemum segetum*: The plant contains coumarins which, if not dried properly, can convert into dicoumarins - an anti-coagulant that causes internal bleeding. Avoid eating leaves raw, especially if dried, just eat the flowers/ petals and fresh young shoots
LOOKALIKES:	For *Chrysanthemum coronarium*: no known hazards BUT as these are so closely related, I would follow the same cautions
MONTH SPAN:	Flowers June - September
FOOD IDEAS:	Chop suey greens, also known as chrysanthemum greens, are widely consumed in Asian cuisine. You can eat the young stems and leaves steamed, stir fried, etc. As the stems grow, they can become stringy so try the stems and discard if necessary, using the tender leaves. The flavour is quite fresh and herby, and stands up well to strong flavours such as garlic and chilli. The petals have a really mushroom-like flavour.

SIMPLE WOK CHOP -SUEY GREENS
(Side veg)

Wok oil/peanut oil for frying
3 stems young chop suey greens
½ tsp chilli flakes
I garlic clove, peeled and finely sliced
¾ inch peeled ginger, sliced into matchstick pieces
½ tsp coriander seed
I dessert spoon toasted sesame oil
(seasoning/soya sauce)

Heat the oil in the wok until hot. Be prepared to work quickly so have everything ready. Add the greens, chilli flakes and coriander seed, tossing or stirring for 30 seconds then add the garlic and ginger, and take off the heat as soon as they start to colour before they burn. Add the sesame oil, toss through and serve. Season if necessary.

OTHER INFO:

I really like the taste of meadowsweet, especially munching on the leaves when I'm out on a walk. Jo described it as Dettol or the smell of pink sticky plasters when you're a kid - I can definitely taste that, as well as that slightly bitter aspirin taste as this plant contains salicylic acid (aspirin is acetyl salicylic acid). Paracelsus and the doctrine of signatures suggested where something grows alludes to the properties it has, so if something grows in temperate cold damp places it aids illnesses caused by such places like colds, flu, rheumatism, etc. and the plant helps - think Aloes in hot places, burns.

MEADOWSWEET SORBET

20-30 meadowsweet flower heads
750g caster sugar
2 lemons
1ltr water

Shake the flower heads (to remove insects) and put in a bowl. Zest the lemons and juice them, putting zest and juice in the bowl with the flower heads. In a saucepan, add the sugar and water and heat to a gentle simmer until the sugar has dissolved. Pour into the bowl with the flower heads and lemon. Cling film the bowl and leave it overnight. Strain the liquid either into a freeze-proof container or into an ice cream maker. If you don't have an ice cream maker, put a lid on your container, pop in the freezer for a couple of hours, take out and mash up with a fork and repeat. To get it really smooth, you can blitz it in a food processor.

MEADOWSWEET

Mead sweet
Filipendula ulmaria

SYNONYM:	*Spiraea ulmaria, Ulmaria pentapetala*
NAME ORIGIN:	Meadowsweet was the blue print for aspirin – the synonym *Spiraea* giving the 'spir' to 'aspirin'. *Filipendula* comes from the Latin *filum* meaning thread and *pendulus* meaning hanging describing the roots. *Ulmaria* means resembles elms (*Ulmus* sp.)
FAMILY:	Rosaceae
EDIBLE PART:	Flowers, leaves
EDIBILITY RATING:	3
WHERE IT'S FOUND:	Wet ground, ditches, meadows, woodland, riversides
CAUTIONS:	Not to be used on children under 12 years old due to salicylate content (risk of Reye's syndrome). Avoid if asthmatic.
MONTH SPAN:	hz 2) flowers June - August (seeds ripen August - September) Summer - late autumn

FOOD IDEAS:	Use the flowers and leaves as a natural sweetener for stewing fruits such as rhubarb, apples, etc. Try making a tea from the flowers or leaves – this is useful for colds and fevers. Meadowsweet cordial/syrup, meadowsweet sorbet...

SAND HOPPER

Talitrus saltator

NAME ORIGIN:	**The species name *saltator* comes from the Latin word meaning 'leaper' or 'dancer', because of the way these creatures hop about.**
FAMILY:	**Talitridae**

EDIBLE PART:	Meat
EDIBILITY RATING:	3
WHERE IT'S FOUND:	Sandy beaches, especially at night if you have lit a fire.
CAUTIONS:	None known - avoid if allergic to shellfish.
MONTH SPAN:	They reproduce from May- August and they live for about 2 years and can overwinter deep in the sand high up the beach.

FOOD IDEAS:	To catch them, light a fire on said beach and watch them cook themselves! Shrimpy and crunchy.
OTHER INFO:	Sand hoppers eat rotting sea vegetation and can strip a freshly caught fish to the bone very fast if left on the sand! When I collect seaweed, I check through it while I collect it, but these little guys hide well. Once I've roasted the seaweed, I'll find these delicious pink mini shrimp-like treats ready cooked. In 2012, scientists from The National Institute of Water and Atmospheric Research (NIWA) from Aberdeen in Scotland found giant sand hoppers 7000 metres deep in the Kermadec trench, north of New Zealand, the largest measuring about 30 cm in length. I'm torn between 'mmmm yum' and 'yikes, I wouldn't want to come face to face with one!'.

MINT JULEP
• (Serves 2)

2 tsp caster sugar
4 springs of apple mint
100ml bourbon
Crushed ice

In each glass, muddle 1 tsp caster sugar and 1 spring of mint. Pour 50ml bourbon in each glass and stir well to dissolve the sugar then top up with crushed ice. Serve with a sprig of apple mint.

APPLE MINT
Mentha x villosa alopecuroides

SYNONYM:	*Mentha x rotundifolia*
NAME ORIGIN:	*Menthe* is the name of a sweet-smelling Greek nymph and *rotundifolia* means round leaves. *Villosa* means shaggy and *alopecuroides* means like a foxtail grass (called *Alopecurus*)
FAMILY:	**Lamiaceae**
EDIBLE PART:	Leaves
EDIBILITY RATING:	4
WHERE IT'S FOUND:	Damp areas, roadsides, ditches, herb gardens
CAUTIONS:	Many of the *Mentha* genera contain oils that can cause abortions, so avoid during pregnancy
MONTH SPAN:	(hz 5) flowers August – September

FOOD IDEAS:	Leaves fresh or dried, raw or cooked. Good for mint sauce, tea, cocktails, desserts, sorbets, chutneys, use roughly chopped as a flavouring.
OTHER INFO:	A cooling herb which can stimulate hair follicles in shampoos, aid digestion and cool fevers and headaches. Do not plant mint in your garden without some way of preventing it spreading – either grow the plant in its pot sunk in the ground or keep it in a pot on your patio/balcony.

CHANTERELLE OR GIROLLE

Cantharellus cibarius

FAMILY:	**Cantharellaceae**
EDIBLE PART:	Mushroom
EDIBILITY RATING:	5
WHERE IT'S FOUND:	Beech, oak, pine woodland (quite often in moss)
CAUTIONS:	Must be cooked as can cause stomach upsets.
LOOKALIKES:	False chanterelle *Hygrophoropsis aurantiaca* is more orange (chanterelles are more yellow), more symmetrical and quite tasteless but luckily edible (just not great!). A way to check if you've found a chanterelle is to press its 'gills' (less gills more folds) – they should 'melt' into the stem rather than break, and they also run down the stem (decurrent). Another lookalike is Jack O'Lantern (I named my first cat Jacko after Jack O'Lanterns as we got him on Hallowe'en and he was all black - my very own witch's cat!) *Omphalotus illudens*, which is poisonous. It is quite rare in the British Isles and mostly grows on dead oak stumps. Winter chanterelle (aka trumpet chanterelles or yellowfoot) *Cantharellus tubaeformis* is similar but is found in autumn to winter. It is edible, prolific and they grow in clumps.
MONTH SPAN:	Late summer - late autumn
FOOD IDEAS:	Sauté in butter, bake in creamy sauces, in chicken dishes, good with rice or pasta but not great with potatoes (maybe I haven't found the right recipe!). Sauté and freeze - they keep their flavour. They can also be pickled.

Chanterelles can be dried to preserve them. These are delicious mushrooms that have a mild sweet flavour almost like baked bread and they hold their firm shape well when cooked. Never ask a forager where their chanterelle spot is… they will never tell.

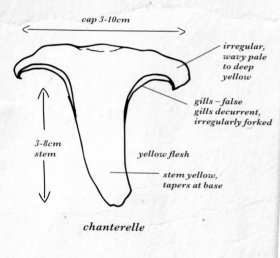

cap 3-10cm

irregular, wavy pale to deep yellow

gills – false gills decurrent, irregularly forked

3-8cm stem

yellow flesh

stem yellow, tapers at base

chanterelle

Winter Chanterelle

SIMPLE SAUTÉED GIROLLES

1 tbsp butter
1 tbsp olive oil
Seasoning
up to 2 good handfuls of girolles
6 sprigs of thyme
1 shallot peeled and finely diced

Put the olive oil and butter in a pan and heat gently on a medium heat. When the butter is melted and sizzling add the shallot to sweat and the thyme. When the shallot has softened, add the girolles and toss to coat. Sauté for 5 to 10 minutes, then serve either with bread or toast, salad and season.
You could add crème fraiche or cream at the end if you wish and toss it through cooked pasta, perhaps with a squeeze of lemon juice.

MAGNOLIA

Magnolia sp.

NAME ORIGIN:	**Named after the French botanist Pierre Magnol.**
FAMILY:	**Magnoliaceae**

EDIBLE PART:	Petals
EDIBILITY RATING:	4
WHERE IT'S FOUND:	In gardens
MONTH SPAN:	Magnolias are split into early flowering and late flowering. If there hasn't been a hard frost some of the early flowering magnolias can be as early as February. The late flowering magnolias can flower into August. Early flowering *Magnolia stellata* is a pretty white flowered species which flowers from March to April, *Magnolia soulangeana* flowers April to May and a beautiful late flowering species is *Magnolia sieboldii* which flowers from May to August.

FOOD IDEAS:	The flavour can vary between a bitter chicory and sweet ginger, depending on the variety – try any magnolia petal to test its flavour. Use the petals fresh as a canape 'boat', pickled like Japanese pickled ginger, made into a syrup, steeped in vinegar or dried until paper-dry and grind up for a ginger-like spice.
OTHER INFO:	If you wish to see one of the 4 National Collections of Magnolias, head to Caerhays Castle on the Roseland in Cornwall, set in such a stunning location by Porthluney Beach. Magnolias come in many different shapes and sizes, including both deciduous and evergreen species. The other National Collections are at Wentworth Castle in Yorkshire, Windsor Great Park in Berkshire and Bodnant in North Wales.

MAGNOLIA SYRUP

35 pink Magnolia petals
1 cup sugar
½ cup water

Put all the ingredients in a saucepan and heat on a medium heat, mashing the petals down (be careful as the liquid will be very hot). Once it is simmering, reduce the temperature to a low simmer for 10 minutes. Take it off the heat and leave it to cool and infuse. Use on porridge, to make drinks, drizzled over ice cream, etc.

LAVENDER SUGAR

500g caster sugar
2-3 tbsp dried lavender buds

Grind the flower buds in a pestle and mortar - they have to be thoroughly dry or the sugar will clump and go mouldy. Stir the lavender and sugar together and leave for 3 days to infuse. Use to make cakes, scones, puddings, etc.

LAVENDER AND LEMON ZEST ICE CREAM

This one's for you, Pat Smith!

2-3 tbsp lavender leaves or
flower heads
zest of 1 lemon
300ml milk
300ml double cream
6 egg yolks
150g caster sugar

Put the milk and cream in a saucepan with the lavender and lemon zest and heat gently. Don't worry about finely zesting the lemon as this will be sieved out. As the liquid is about to simmer, take off the heat and leave to infuse until cool. In a large bowl, beat together the sugar and egg yolks until pale and creamy. Reheat the milk/cream infusion until about to simmer, pass it through a sieve into the yolks, whisking well, then return to the saucepan. Keep stirring constantly (on a medium low temperature) and when the mixture has thickened enough to coat the back of the spoon, remove from the heat and freeze. If you don't have an ice cream maker, freeze for a couple of hours, break up the mixture (and ice crystals) with a fork, then return to the freezer, repeating the process one more time.

LAVENDER
Lavandula angustifolia

SYNONYM:	*Lavandula officinale*
NAME ORIGIN:	*Lavare* means 'to wash' in French, *Lavo* is 'I wash' in Latin. Freshly washed clothes were hung on lavender bushes to scent them as they dried, people bathed in lavender scented baths as it is an excellent healer. *Angustifolia* means narrow leaved and *officinale* means of the apothecary shop (medicinal).
FAMILY:	Lamiaceae

EDIBLE PART:	Flowers, leaves
EDIBILITY RATING:	4
WHERE IT'S FOUND:	Gardens, garden escape, dry slopes
CAUTIONS:	Lavender essential oil is one of the only ones that can be applied directly to skin (almost all others need to be diluted first with a carrier oil), although it rarely causes sensitization
MONTH SPAN:	Evergreen herb, flowers from July - September (hz 5)

FOOD IDEAS:	Lavender crème brulée, lavender shortbread, cupcakes, lavender and lemon zest ice cream, vinaigrettes, with lamb, jelly, goes well with goat's cheese, try with earl grey flavoured cakes. Use the leaves when the flowers aren't in bloom as they flavour dishes just as well.
OTHER INFO:	Lavender is one of the best antiseptics and anti-inflammatory essential oils, which was used in hospitals in WWI to give relief to burns, bites and inflamed skin conditions. Also helps to aid sleep, but too much and it can cause headaches.

AGRIMONY

Agrimonia eupatoria

SYNONYM:	*Agrimonia odorata*
NAME ORIGIN:	*Eupatoria* is named after Mithridates Eupator, a Pontine Emperor who was an expert in herbal therapy. *Agrimonia* comes from the Greek *argemone* meaning poppy, probably deriving from ager which is Latin for field.
FAMILY:	**Rosaceae**
EDIBLE PART:	Leaves, flowers, seed
EDIBILITY RATING:	2
WHERE IT'S FOUND:	Verges, fields, meadows, sunny walls, hedgerows
CAUTIONS:	High in tannins which can cause constipation
MONTH SPAN:	Flowers from June - August, seeds ripen August - September

FOOD IDEAS:	You can make a tea made from aerial parts (fresh or dried), the seeds can be used dried and ground down to add to flour, etc.
OTHER INFO:	Agrimony has been used medicinally to stop bleeding, to heal ulcers and for treating gallstones. In the Victorian 'Language of Flowers' agrimony is used to represent thankfulness and gratitude.

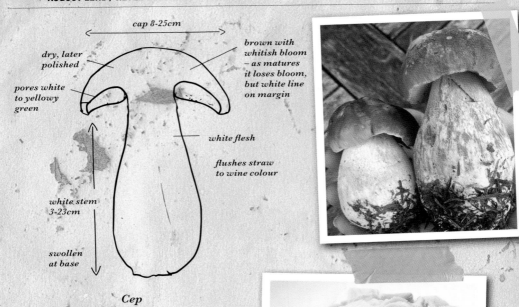

cap 8-25cm

dry, later
polished

brown with
whitish bloom
– as matures
it loses bloom,
but white line
on margin

pores white
to yellowy
green

white flesh

flushes straw
to wine colour

white stem
3-23cm

swollen
at base

Cep

CEPS
WITH PAPPARDELLE
AND PINE NUTS
(serves 4)

1/4 cup olive oil
6 small to medium sized ceps
1 finely chopped shallot
1 finely chopped clove of garlic
1 good handful of parsley
1 good handful pine nuts
pappardelle pasta for 4 (800g)
100ml crème fraiche or double cream
Seasoning

Boil the pasta and cook until al dente. Wipe if necessary and slice up the ceps. Dry toast the pine nuts and put to one side. In a frying pan, heat the olive oil to a medium heat. Add the shallots and when softened add the ceps, tossing until golden and add the garlic near the end to prevent burning. Add the parsley, cream or crème fraiche and seasoning, simmer, stir in the pasta and pine nuts and serve.

CEP, BOLETE
Boletus edulis

NAME ORIGIN:	*Edulis* means edible and *Boletus* comes from the Latin term for mushroom. Originally *bolos* means lump or clod and in Ancient Greek it means terrestrial fungus.
FAMILY:	**Boletaceae**
EDIBLE PART:	Mushroom
EDIBILITY RATING:	5
WHERE IT'S FOUND:	Beech, oak, birch, conifer trees, woodland - open areas
LOOKALIKES:	Bitter bolete *Tylopilus felleus* - not poisonous but very bitter and will ruin a dish if you cook with them. It has dark striations on the stem and a pinkish colour to the pores.
MONTH SPAN:	Summer – autumn

OTHER INFO:	Warning! May contain maggots! A good time to look for boletes is when you've had fairly dry weather for a while and then a good downpour, wait 1 week and then go hunting!

FLAX, LINSEED
Linum usitatissimum

SYNONYM:	*Linum indehiscens, Linum humile, Linum crepitans*
NAME ORIGIN:	*Usitatissimum* means extremely useful! *Linum* gives its name to Linoleic acid which is obtained from the plant (oils from seeds) and is used to make lino (linoleum) flooring.
FAMILY:	**Linaceae**

EDIBLE PART:	Seed
EDIBILITY RATING:	3
WHERE IT'S FOUND:	Wild flower escape, cultivated
CAUTIONS:	Avoid during pregnancy or if you suffer from prostate gland diseases, the seeds contain prussic acid (hydrogen cyanide) which in small doses improves digestion and stimulates respiration but avoid taking in large doses or drinking water whilst eating.
MONTH SPAN:	Flowers June - July, seeds ripen August - September

FOOD IDEAS:	Seeds in bread, in salads, sprouted
OTHER INFO:	Flaxseed oil is a drying oil which is used in carpentry for treating wood and also in painting with oil paints as it helps pigments combine.

GRILLED HERRING WITH DILL MAYO ON WATERCRESS

(serves 2)

4 herring fillets (bones removed)
olive oil
juice of 1/2 a lemon
1 tbsp fresh finely chopped dill
2-3 tbsp mayonnaise
1 tsp Dijon mustard
washed watercress
seasoning

Pop the fillets on a lightly oiled baking tray, rub a little olive oil on the fillets with a little seasoning and pop under the grill, checking and turning until the flesh is cooked through and the skin is crisp. For the mayonnaise, mix the mayo, dill, lemon juice and mustard together in a bowl and thin it slightly with a little olive oil. Taste and season accordingly. Put the watercress on plates, lay 2 fillets crisp side up on the watercress, drizzle olive oil over the fish and watercress, then either top or put the mayo on the side.

HERRING

Silver darlings
Clupea sp.

NAME ORIGIN:	**The word herring comes from the Old Germanic for multitude because they were once in abundance. The word *Clupea* means anchovy in Latin.**
FAMILY:	**Clupeidae**
EDIBLE PART:	Meat
EDIBILITY RATING:	5
WHERE IT'S FOUND:	Mostly off shore, with mackerel hooks, occasionally from piers
CAUTIONS:	Limit your intake to twice a week at the most as these fish can contain heavy metals due to pollution and what they eat - oily fish is very good for you, for skin, hair and general health as it is high in vitamins, omega-3 fatty acids and protein
MONTH SPAN:	All year around – different stocks of herring spawn at different times of the year. It is classed as least endangered.

FOOD IDEAS:	Grilled, fried, poached, smoked, marinated or soused. Try rollmops - filleted herrings that are pickled and wrapped into a spiral and pinned with a toothpick, sometimes with a savoury filling. Kippers are split (gutted) and cold smoked herring.
OTHER INFO:	Mum and Dad moved to Holland with my older brother and sister in 1971 (before moving to Canada and having me!). Dad was slow at learning Dutch but would give it a go, whereas Mum was excellent at grammar and picking up languages fairly quickly. After a few mishaps like buying yoghurt thinking it was milk, or asking for a cut of bread and being told she was asking for a French chicken, they soon got the hang of it and loved all the new foody challenges that lay before them. Once Mum was out with a neighbour and they bought herring which typically you would eat as street food, but Mum couldn't face that and brought it back home to eat. When Mum and Dad tried it, they loved it and this became one of their favourite snacks, along with Jenever (Dutch gin).

EUROPEAN PILCHARD

Sardine
Sardina pilchardus

NAME ORIGIN:	**Possibly named after Sardinia where these fish were once plentiful.**
FAMILY:	**Clupeidae**
EDIBLE PART:	Meat
EDIBILITY RATING:	5
WHERE IT'S FOUND:	Sea, off boat
CAUTIONS:	None known – avoid if allergic to fish, beware of small bones as they are a choking hazard
LOOKALIKES:	These fish are in the herring family and when you buy a tin of sardines, they could be one of up to twenty-one species. Sardines have a silver belly, golden sides and a green tone along their upper parts.
MONTH SPAN:	July - March
FOOD IDEAS:	Smoked, salted, dried, pan fried, grilled, barbequed and on toast!
OTHER INFO:	Sardines are high in vitamin B and protein and low in calories. Caught with nets or traps and at night is best as they feed on plankton which draws them up to the surface. The adults are often classed as pilchards and the juveniles as sardines. Quite recently they have been sold as 'Cornish Sardines'. Around Cornwall you can find remnants of old pilchard works such as at Portgiskey near Mevagissey.

> "Here's health to the Pope, may he live to repent
> And add just six months to the term of his Lent
> And tell all his vassals from Rome to the Poles,
> There's nothing like pilchards for saving their souls!"

STARGAZEY PIE
(serves 4)

1 tbsp butter
1 tbsp olive oil
1 onion finely chopped
3 rashers of bacon finely chopped - optional
or 1 tsp Dijon mustard
1/2 tbsp flour
3 tbsp white wine
250ml veg or fish stock
300ml double cream
1 tbsp finely chopped chervil or tarragon
Seasoning
2 eggs - boiled, shelled and chopped
6 pilchards
200g puff pastry
milk or egg yolk for brushing the pastry

De-scale, gut and fillet the fish, removing the bones but keeping the tails and heads. Preheat the oven to 200 degrees C. In a saucepan, heat the butter and the oil and fry the onion. Add the bacon if you are using it and fry, otherwise add the flour and using a balloon whisk, slowly add the wine and stock to prevent lumps. Simmer for 10 minutes allowing it to reduce, then add the cream and mustard if using it and continue to simmer until the mixture has thickened. Take off the heat and add the herbs and boiled egg, stir and season to taste. In a pie dish, lay the fillets on the bottom, cover with the sauce and top the dish with rolled out puff pastry, using a little milk or egg to wet the rim of the dish. Make slits in the pastry and push through the fish heads and tails for decoration, so that the heads are facing 'the stars'. Brush the pastry with the rest of the milk or egg yolk and bake in the oven for about 40 minutes or until the pastry is golden. Serve with new potatoes (preferably Cornish as this is a Cornish dish!) and greens or salad.

CHERRY PLUM

Myrobalan plum
Prunus cerasifera

SYNONYM:	*Prunus domestica myrobalan*
NAME ORIGIN:	*Prunus* is the classic name for plum and *cerasifera* potentially comes from *cera* meaning wax and *fera* wild.
FAMILY:	Rosaceae

EDIBLE PART:	Fruits
EDIBILITY RATING:	4
WHERE IT'S FOUND:	Sun or semi shade, hedging, car parks
CAUTIONS:	The leaves and seed contain hydrogen cyanide, so don't eat! It is okay to consume small quantities of it, but the ripe fruit is the best bit!
MONTH SPAN:	Flowers in March, fruits ripen from August - September (hz 4)

FOOD IDEAS:	Fruits are sweet and delicious raw or cooked - wine, liqueur, jam, cakes, pies, sauces
OTHER INFO:	the fruits can remain on the tree until Oct. I really REALLY want my own beautiful trees so I can pick loads and make wine or a liqueur from them! Cherry plums are native to Eurasia where they are often picked before they are ripe and red but green and sour, then dipped in salt as a snack.

CHERRY PLUM CORDIAL

500g cherry plums
100g -170g caster sugar
1ltr water

Put the cherry plums and water into a saucepan and simmer gently until the cherry plums have softened and gone pulpy. Get a container such as a large jug, put the cherry plum pulp into a muslin bag and let it drip into the jug, preferably for 24 hours. Do not be tempted to squeeze the bag as the cordial will go cloudy. In a clean saucepan put the cherry plum liquid and add the least amount of sugar, stirring as you go to check the sweetness. Add more if you need to. Heat on a low temperature until the sugar has dissolved then pour into sterilized bottles. Keeps for a couple of months.

FUCHSIA BERRY JAM

450g jam sugar (with added pectin)
1 lemon
525g fuchsia berries
2 tbsp water

Put the water and sugar into a saucepan and squeeze in the juice from the lemon. Heat gently until the sugar has dissolved. Take the saucepan off the heat and leave to cool. Once cool, tip in the berries without any stalks (don't stir) and return to the heat. Bring to the boil and do the cold plate test to see when it has set. Store in sterilized jars.

FUCHSIA

Fuchsia sp.

NAME ORIGIN:	**Named after the German botanist Leonhart Fuchs.**
FAMILY:	**Onagraceae**

EDIBLE PART:	Flowers, fruits (some of the best are *F. magellanica, F. corymbiflora, F. excorticata, F. boliviana, F. splendens, F. fulgens, F. coccinea* and *F.* 'Fuchsiaberry'
EDIBILITY RATING:	1-4
WHERE IT'S FOUND:	Gardens, garden escape
MONTH SPAN:	June – Oct, fruits July – Oct (different species)

FOOD IDEAS:	Use the flowers to decorate cakes, etc. They can also be crystallized like primroses and violets. The fruits vary in taste including some that taste like watermelon sweets, some lemony, some insipid and others which are sweet but peppery. Try them raw first and decide which would be good for making jam. To drink the nectar, pinch off the green ovary at the base of the flower and suck the base of the remaining flower (sometimes pulling out the stigma will bring out a droplet of nectar). Other ideas are fuchsia berry sauce, added to cakes, muffins, etc.
OTHER INFO:	Fuchsias remind me of 2 things – when I was about 4 at Lensbury Club in Teddington where my Mum's cousins Kathleen and Gordon showed me how to drink the nectar from them. Secondly my foraging walks at Heligan Gardens near St. Austell, where I'd show my group the fruits and watch their reactions; firstly being able to eat fuchsia berries and the second on the peppery kick that sets some people off coughing (me included!). The majority of fuchsias come from South America and are tropical or subtropical.

RUSSULAS, CHARCOAL BURNER, BRITTLEGILLS

Russula sp.

NAME ORIGIN:	*Russula* comes from the word 'russet' meaning red. Many russulas are red, which are the more difficult ones to identify.
FAMILY:	**Russulaceae**
EDIBLE PART:	Mushroom
EDIBILITY RATING:	3
WHERE IT'S FOUND:	Mostly woodlands, broad wood, beech, oak, occasionally birch
CAUTIONS:	None known, see lookalikes
LOOKALIKES:	Charcoal burner *Russula cyanoxantha*, powdery brittlegill *Russula parazurea*, greencracked brittlegill *Russula virescens* are the best to try and identify out of all the russulas. They have greenish caps including charcoal burner but this can have a cap in white, yellow, pink or even purple! This is the only one that doesn't have brittle gills but instead has soft and flexible gills. Try nibbling a tiny bit and spit out if it is bitter, hot or just plain vile!
	The sickener *Russula emetica* can cause vomiting and gastrointestinal problems so avoid – this has a red cap and a very hot flavour. Russulas look similar to *Lactarius* species which exude milk (russulas don't). *Russula* gills are brittle and decurrent which means the gills run down the stem. Amanitas look similar but have free gills which stop at the stem and don't run down it. Russulas don't have a ring or a skirt on the stem, but they do have white gills.
MONTH SPAN:	Summer - autumn

Slice and fry or sauté with garlic, goes well with lemon, they are pretty firm mushrooms and hold their shape well. Peel if you are eating them raw, bake, grill or stuff them. They go well with tomatoes, as bruschetta or in mushroom en croûte.

cap 5-15cm

varying colours

cap globose later flattening to depressed centre

white flesh

gills adnexed to slightly decurrent white to pale cream

white stem

Russulas

RUSSULA SLICES

1 block of puff pastry (225g)
1 tbsp olive oil
1 tbsp butter
175g russulas, cleaned and sliced
4 leeks washed and sliced
2 cloves of garlic, peeled and minced
1 tsp mixed herbs
75g grated cheese
50g toasted flaked almonds (can use pine nuts)
1 splash of sherry
Seasoning
milk to glaze

Preheat the oven to 200 degrees C. Roll out the pastry and cut in 2 or 4 pieces (you will fold over half to make the pastry slices). Put the pastry onto a greased baking tray (with parchment on). Heat the oil and butter in a frying pan and gently fry the leeks until tender. Add the mushrooms and fry for 5 minutes then add the remaining ingredients, simmering for a further 5 minutes. Put the mixture onto half of the pastry and pull the bare half of the pastry over and seal the edge with milk. Prick the top with a fork or with a sharp knife, glaze the top with milk and bake for 20-25 minutes until golden. For a slight variation, you can add cream or crème fraiche in the mix just before putting in the pastry and baking for a creamy mushroom slice.

SALTY FINGERS
Batis maritima

NAME ORIGIN:	**Unsure of origin but *Batis* seems to relate to saltwort plants including *Salicornia*, and *maritima* means of the sea**
FAMILY:	**Bataceae**

EDIBLE PART:	Succulent parts
EDIBILITY RATING:	3
WHERE IT'S FOUND:	Coastal regions, exposed sites, salt marshes
MONTH SPAN:	All year round

FOOD IDEAS:	Eat them raw or lightly steamed, pickled, sautéed, deep fried, good in pasta dishes, as a garnish. It is salty and slightly bitter and goes well with meat, fish, shellfish and mushrooms.
OTHER INFO:	This plant is found only sporadically in the UK but thrives where it grows. It is classed as an invasive species in places like Hawaii. I have been trying to find this plant for years and I finally found it, growing in a place I have visited many times before!

HIMALAYAN BALSAM

Jewelweed
Impatiens glandulifera

SYNONYM:	*Impatiens roylei*
NAME ORIGIN:	The Latin word *Impatiens* means impatient referring to the exploding seeds, *glandis* means gland and *ferre* means to bear… gland-bearing referring to the leaves. The plant originates from the Himalayan mountains, hence the common name.
FAMILY:	Balsaminaceae

EDIBLE PART:	Seed, flowers, young leaves and shoots, unripe seed pods (all need to be cooked except the seeds)
EDIBILITY RATING:	4
WHERE IT'S FOUND:	Waste ground, roadsides, riverbanks
CAUTIONS:	Avoid if you suffer from gout, arthritis, rheumatism, kidney stones. Avoid eating too often because of the high mineral content, although cooking or drying destroys the harmful minerals.
MONTH SPAN:	Flowers August - October, seeds ripen late August - November

FOOD IDEAS:	Raw or toasted seeds made into veggie burgers, cookies, bread, pastries. The flowers make an excellent cerise pink jam. Try the cooked young leaves and shoots and the cooked unripe seed pods.
OTHER INFO:	The seed pods are cleverly engineered spring loaded mini-bombs, where the slightest touch will set them off! They are related to busy Lizzies and were introduced to the UK at the same time as Japanese knotweed.

HIMALAYAN
BALSAM COOKIES

2 cups butter
1 2/3 cups sugar
2 1/3 cups flour
2 cups toasted Himalayan balsam seeds
60ml cold water

Preheat the oven to 150 degrees C. Cream the butter and sugar together, then add the remaining ingredients. Roll out to about half a centimetre thick, cut out shapes and bake for about 10 minutes. Dust with icing sugar or any other decorations you wish.

RECIPE:	This doesn't require an actual recipe but something worth trying is ugni gin. Make it the same way you would sloe gin with sugar, gin and ugni berries. Combine, shake occasionally and leave it for a couple of months.
OTHER INFO:	Originally from Chile, this has become a popular garden plant and makes excellent evergreen hedges laden with fruits.

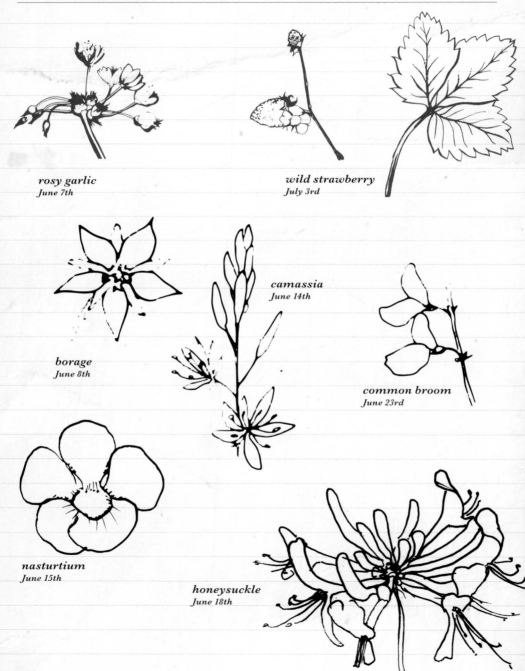

rosy garlic
June 7th

wild strawberry
July 3rd

borage
June 8th

camassia
June 14th

common broom
June 23rd

nasturtium
June 15th

honeysuckle
June 18th

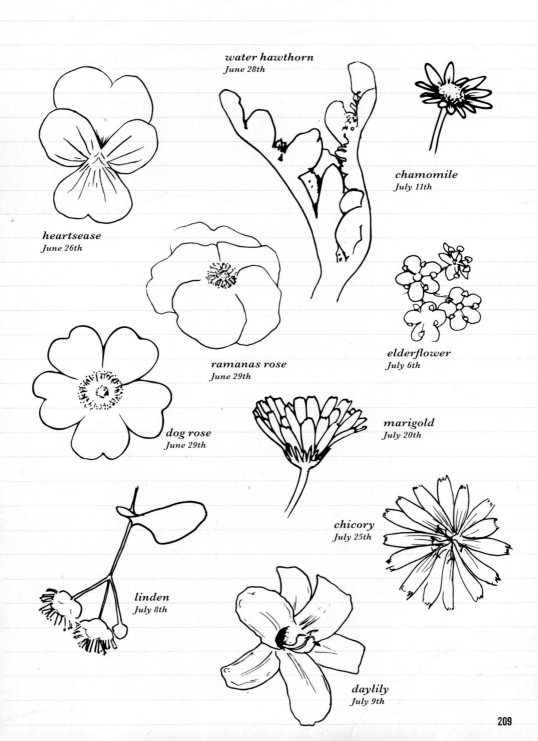

water hawthorn
June 28th

chamomile
July 11th

heartsease
June 26th

ramanas rose
June 29th

elderflower
July 6th

dog rose
June 29th

marigold
July 20th

chicory
July 25th

linden
July 8th

daylily
July 9th

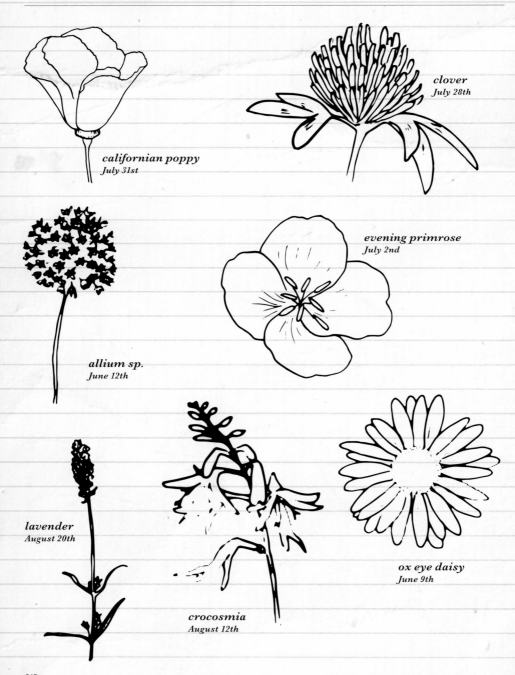

californian poppy
July 31st

clover
July 28th

allium sp.
June 12th

evening primrose
July 2nd

lavender
August 20th

crocosmia
August 12th

ox eye daisy
June 9th

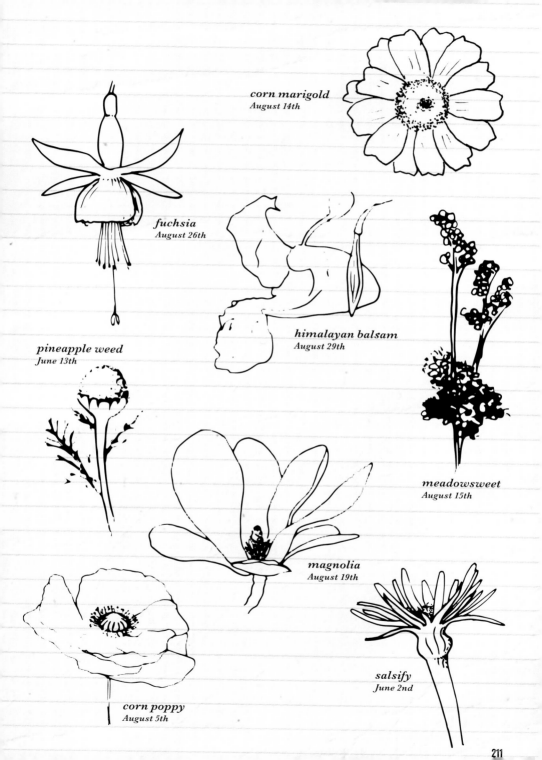

corn marigold
August 14th

fuchsia
August 26th

himalayan balsam
August 29th

pineapple weed
June 13th

meadowsweet
August 15th

magnolia
August 19th

corn poppy
August 5th

salsify
June 2nd

MEDICAL TERMINOLOGY

abortifacient
(Chiefly of a drug) causing abortion.

acetic acid
The acid that gives vinegar its characteristic taste. The pure acid is a colourless viscous liquid or glassy solid. Alternative name: ethanoic acid; chemical formula: CH_3COOH

alkaloids
Any of a class of nitrogenous organic compounds of plant origin which have pronounced physiological actions on humans. They include many drugs (morphine, quinine) and poisons (atropine, strychnine).

anthocyanin
A blue, violet, or red flavonoid pigment found in plants.

anticoagulant
Having the effect of retarding or inhibiting the coagulation of the blood.

arthritis
A serious condition in which a person's joints become painful, swollen and stiff.

bio-mimicry
The design and production of materials, structures, and systems that are modelled on biological entities and processes.

carcinogens
A substance capable of causing cancer in living tissue.

coumarins
A vanilla-scented compound found in many plants, formerly used for flavouring food. A bicyclic lactone; chemical formula: $C_9H_6O_2$

dermatitis
A medical condition in which the skin becomes red, swollen, and sore, sometimes with small blisters, resulting from direct irritation of the skin by an external agent or an allergic reaction to it.

di-coumarins (dicoumarins)
Dicoumarin is a crystalline compound that is naturally formed from damp spoiled plants in the pea family (Fabaceae) which smelled sweet due to containing coumarins. Dicoumarin is a potent anticoagulant which if eaten causes spontaneous haemorrhaging.

emmenagogue
A substance that stimulates or increases menstrual flow.

erucic
It is present in all sorts incl pastries, etc because it can be found in vegetable oil. Don't let young children consume in large quantities.

erucic acid (Brassicaceae)
A solid compound present in mustard and rape seeds. An unsaturated fatty acid: chemical formula: $C_{21}H_{41}COOH$

farnesol
A natural compound present in many essential oils such as rose, citronella and tuberose which when isolated is used in the perfume industry to enhance sweet floral fragrances.

furocoumarins
Chemical substances that cause skin sensitivity to sunlight, which leave irregular pigmentation and skin prone to sunburn.

galactose
A sugar of the hexose class which is a constituent of lactose and many polysaccharides.

gamma-linolenic acid (GLA)
A polyunsaturated fatty acid (with one more double bond than linoleic acid) present as a glyceride in linseed and other oils and essential in the human diet.

gout
A build up of uric acid.

hydrogen cyanide
A highly poisonous gas or volatile liquid with an odour of bitter almonds, made by the action of acids on cyanides. Chemical formula: HCN

hypothyroidism
Abnormally low activity of the thyroid gland, resulting in retardation of growth and mental development in children and adults.

oxalic acid
A poisonous crystalline acid with a sour taste, present in rhubarb leaves, wood sorrel, and other plants. Alternative name: **ethanedioic acid**; chemical formula: $(COOH)_2$

phenothiazines
A synthetic compound which is used in veterinary medicine to treat parasitic infestations of animals. A heterocyclic compound; chemical formula: $C_{12}H_9NS$

photosensitivity
To have a chemical, electrical or other response to light.

pyrrolizidine alkaloids
A group of alkaloids produced by certain plant families to protect the plant from insect herbivore damage. Over consuming can cause liver damage and damage to other organs. It can also be a potential cause of cancer.

reye's (reye) syndrome
A rare but serious disorder that causes swelling in the liver and brain, affecting children and young adults, often who are recovering from a viral infection.

rheumatism
A medical condition that causes stiffness and pain in the joints or muscles of the body.

saponins
A toxic compound which is present in certain plants such as soapwort and makes foam when shaken with water.

sedative
A drug used to calm a person or animal or to make them sleep.

thiaminase
An enzyme that destroys thiamine which is vitamin B1. Deficiency can result in beriberi - a disease that affects systems of the body such as the nervous system and digestive system.

thujone
A chemical with a menthol odour found in certain conifers and plants such as tansy, artemisia and sage. Thujone is a stimulant and convulsant in large quantities.

trimethylamine
An organic compound produced by the decomposition of plants and animals - the smell of death.

trypsin inhibitors
An inhibitor of trypsin - a digestive enzyme which breaks down proteins in the small intestine, secreted by the pancreas as trypsinogen.

FOOD TERMINOLOGY

bain marie
A pan of hot water in which a cooking container is placed for slow cooking.

crudités
Small pieces of uncooked vegetables, often served with a dip before a meal.

en papillote
A food cooked and served in paper.

mirin
A rice wine used as a flavouring in Japanese cookery.

wasabi
A Japanese plant with a thick green root which tastes like strong horseradish and is used in cookery, especially in powder or paste form as an accompaniment to raw fish.

FISH AND SHELLFISH

carapace
The hard upper shell of a tortoise, crustacean, or arachnid.

pelagic
Fish that inhabit the many upper layers of the open sea. Mackerel are pelagic or wandering as they will go in search of food where most fish inhabit one layer and wait for food to come to them so as not to expend too much energy.

PLANT TERMINOLOGY

aerial parts
All parts of a plant growing above the ground.

annual
A plant that lives for a year or less, perpetuating itself by seed.

biennial
A plant that takes two years to grow from seed to fruition and die.

perennial
A plant that lives for several years.

bract
A modified leaf or scale, typically small, with a flower or flower cluster in its axil. Bracts are sometimes larger and more brightly coloured than the true flower, as in poinsettia.

bulbils
A tiny secondary bulb-like structure that can produce new plants.

calyx
The sepals of a flower, typically forming a whorl that encloses the petals and forms a protective layer around a flower in bud.

corymbs - like elderflower
A flower cluster whose lower stalks are proportionally longer so that the flowers form a flat or slightly convex head.

croziers
The curled top of a young fern, named after a hooked staff carried by a bishop.

cultivar
A plant variety that has been produced in cultivation by selective breeding. Cultivars are usually designated in the style *Taxus baccata* 'Variegata'.

endemic
Native, indigenous to a specific place.

family
A principal taxonomic category that ranks above genus and below order, usually ending in *-idae* (in zoology) or *-aceae* (in botany).

genus
A principal taxonomic category that ranks above species and below family, and is denoted by a capitalized Latin name, e.g. *Helianthus*.

glaucous
From the Latin glaucus which means greyish blue or grey, or covered in a fine bloom (such as grapes).

hz - hardiness zone
Hardiness of a plant depends on its ability to survive outside during winter.

sepals
Each of the parts of the calyx of a flower, enclosing the petals and typically green and leaf-like.

silicles
Disc-shaped seed pods of the Brassicaceae family.

species
A group of living organisms consisting of similar individuals capable of exchanging genes or interbreeding. The species is the principal natural taxonomic unit, ranking below a genus and denoted by a Latin binomial, e.g. *Helianthus annuus*.

stamen
The male fertilizing organ of a flower, typically consisting of a pollen-containing anther and a filament.

stigma
In a flower the part of a pistil that receives the pollen during pollination.

stolon
A creeping horizontal plant stem or runner that produces roots at certain points that form new plants, for example strawberries.

synonym
A taxonomic name which has the same application as another, especially one which has been superceded and is no longer valid.

variety
A taxonomic category that ranks below subspecies (where present) or species, its members differing from others of the same subspecies or species in minor but permanent or heritable characteristics. Varieties are more often recognized in botany, in which they are designated in the style *Apium graveolens* (var. **dulce**).

vetiver
A tall fragrant perennial grass native to India (*Chrysopogon zizanoides*) which has a sweet, earthy and woody fragrance.

whorl
A set of leaves, flowers, or branches springing from the stem at the same level and encircling it.

ROOTS

corm
A rounded underground storage organ present in plants such as croci, gladioli, and cyclamens, consisting of a swollen stem base covered with scale leaves.

rhizome
A continuously growing horizontal underground stem which puts out lateral shoots and adventitious roots at intervals.

bulb
A rounded underground storage organ present in some plants, notably those of the lily family, consisting of a short stem surrounded by fleshy scale leaves or leaf bases, lying dormant over winter.

FUNGI

adnate
The gills are attached to the stem.

decurrent
A fungus gill extending down the stem below the point of attachment.

free gills
The gills are not attached to the stem.

adnexed
The gills are narrowly attached to the stem.

emarginate
Gills are notched before attaching to the stem.

seceding
Gills are attached but the edges break away.

sinuate
The gills are smoothly notched before running down the stem.

subdecurrent
The gills run slightly down the stem.

By scientific name A-Z

By common name A – Z

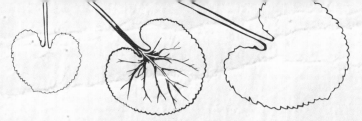

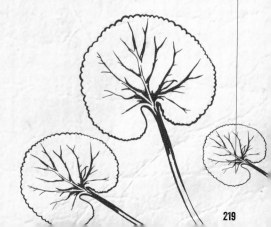

By recipe A-Z

Acknowledgements

Design – Leap www.leap.eco
Illustration – Orlagh Murphy, Emma Gunn
Photographer – Emma Gunn
Proof-readers – Barbara Ball, Emma Gunn

Picture credits
All photos are copyright of Emma Gunn, Shutterstock
Marasmius oreades by
Kerry Woodfield
www.woodfieldwild.com
Ligusticum scoticum by
Lisa Cutcliffe www.eduliswildfood.co.uk
Parietaria Judaica by Barbara Ball

Author photograph by Ben Foster

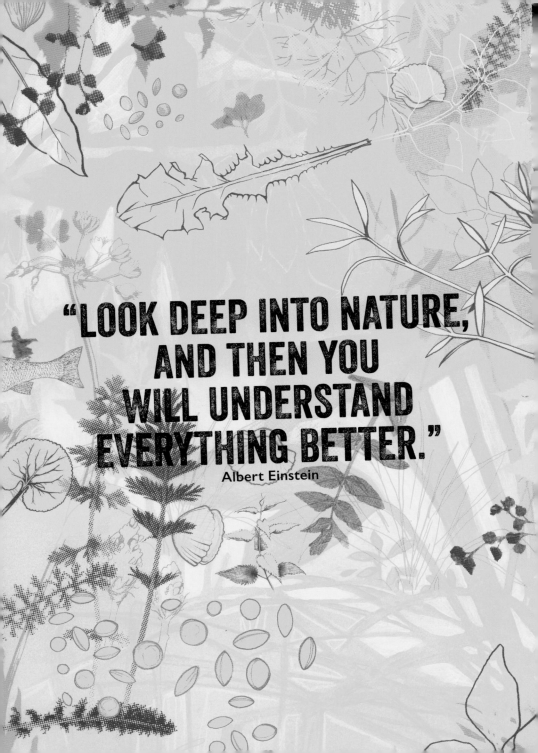

"LOOK DEEP INTO NATURE,
AND THEN YOU
WILL UNDERSTAND
EVERYTHING BETTER."
Albert Einstein